The Foreign Policy Struggle
Congress and the President
in the 1990s and Beyond

Stanley Sloan
Mary Locke
   and
Casimir A. Yost

Institute for the Study of Diplomacy
EDMUND A. WALSH SCHOOL OF FOREIGN SERVICE
GEORGETOWN UNIVERSITY

Note: The views expressed in this report do not necessarily reflect the views of any of the organizations, governmental or private, with which the individual participants in the discussion group are affiliated.

Institute for the Study of Diplomacy
Edmund A. Walsh School of Foreign Service
Georgetown University, Washington, D.C.   20057–1025
© 2000 by the Institute for the Study of Diplomacy.

All rights rerved by the publisher. No part of this Monograph may be reproduced, stored in a retrieval system, or transmitted in any form or by any means—electronic, electrostatic, magnetic tape, mechanical, photocopying, recording, or otherwise—without permission in writing from the Institute for the Study of Diplomacy. Material contained in this Monograph may be quoted with appropriate citation.

ISBN 0-934742-94-4
Printed in the United States of America

Contents

Introduction   vii

1
Findings and Lessons for the Future   1
Findings   1
Lessons   5

2
Congress and Foreign Policy in the 1990s   11
The Past is Prologue   11
A New Era for Foreign Policy-making   13

3
Key Factors   19
Leadership   19
Interest Groups   26
Public Opinion   30
Partisanship   33
Institutions and Processes   37

4
The Cases and their Impact on U.S. Interests   41
Security Policy   42
Trade and International Finance   49
Foreign Policy Tools   52

5
Conclusions   59

Discussion Group Participants   61

Introduction

In recent years, the Institute for the Study of Diplomacy (ISD) has focused significant attention on the functioning of U.S. government foreign policy institutions. The Institute has undertaken studies of the Department of State, the United States Information Agency, the intelligence community, U.S. embassies around the world, and on the resources being expended in support of U.S. foreign policy objectives.

This study focuses on the Congress as an essential actor in the policy making process. In particular, it examines the congressional role in the 1990s, asking the following questions: Has the congressional role changed fundamentally in the post-Cold War decade? Are there lessons that can be drawn from an examination of the interaction between the legislative and executive branches in the 1990s? Finally, based on the experiences of the 1990s, how can constitutionally mandated sharing of power between the branches be improved?

The project builds on excellent recent analyses of the role of Congress and national security policy that can be found in studies by Jeremy D. Rosner, *The New Tug-of-War, Congress, the Executive Branch and National Security* (Washington, D.C.: Carnegie Endowment for International Peace, 1995) and Dov S. Zakheim, *Congress and National Security in the Post-Cold War Era* (Washington, D.C.: The Nixon Center, 1998). Because defense issues are covered by these publications, the ISD project concentrates on the foreign policy side of the foreign and defense policy nexus.

The Institute assembled a discussion group of thirty-five current and former congressional staff, executive branch officials, and academic experts (see the list of participants on page 61). Many group members had decades of experience working in or with the Congress. They represented the major divisions within our body politic: the division between the parties, the splits within the parties, the divide between the House and the Senate, and the separation between the two branches. Despite sharp differences of perspective, they were united by a deep respect for the people and institutions they served and a common concern that the system, while not broken, could be working better.

The members of the discussion group participated in their private capacities, speaking only for themselves. They did not agree on all issues, and this report is not a consensus document. No one was asked to "sign on" to the findings and recommendations. Indeed, some members expressed reservations about several specific points. Instead, the report seeks to reflect the lively and informed discussions that took place over five meetings from November 1998 until October 1999 while capturing some key insights that emerged from the collective inquiry.

Stanley Sloan, who retired in 1999 after more than twenty years with the Congressional Research Service, was the principal drafter of the final report. Mary Locke, who worked in the U.S. Senate from 1976 to 1985, served as project manager and contributed significantly to the final document. School of Foreign Service graduate students Thomas Kim, Michael Garcia, Simon Limage, Kevin Ritz and Marcos Mandojana prepared background material on the cases.

The group met for a planning meeting in November 1998. It was determined at that meeting that the project should focus on ten "cases" of executive-legislative engagement in the 1990s in the foreign policy field. The cases were selected because they were examples of significant interaction between the branches, many or most had their origins in the 1980s or before, and all involved issues that will be on the agendas of future administrations.

The cases chosen were: Nunn-Lugar legislation and Soviet weapons of mass destruction; Bosnia, Kosovo and the use of force; North Atlantic Treaty Organization (NATO) enlargement (based on a separate ISD study of the politics of the issue); U.S. policy toward China; fast-track trade negotiating authority; increasing the International Monetary Fund quota; resources for foreign affairs; State Department reorganization; the Glenn Amendment of 1994 (sanctions to deter nuclear detonations by India and Pakistan); and funding for the United Nations (UN).

In each case, the group considered several key questions:

- How effective was the leadership provided by the President and by the Congress?

- What role did interest groups and/or public opinion play?

- What was the role of partisanship?

- How well did institutional structures work?

Finally, how did the handling of the issue affect overall U.S. foreign policy and national interests?

The planning meeting—and subsequent sessions of the project—grappled particularly with how to define a "successful" outcome. There was recognition that the two branches could agree on policies that did not further the national interest. For some members, the sanctions legislation passed by the Congress in the 1990s and signed by the President fit this category. In several cases, whether or not an outcome was "successful" may not become clear for many years. Generally, however, the group believed that prospects for a successful outcome, that is, one that furthers U.S. national interests, is enhanced when a policy has the support of the President and majorities in both houses.

The group met in February, March, and April 1999 to discuss the cases. Background papers on each case were prepared by the five Georgetown graduate students paired with group members, who subsequently introduced the case to the group.

The discussion group examined an initial draft of the final report at its April meeting. A revised draft was discussed at the group's final meeting in October 1999. Readers should be aware that this report, while taking into account a substantial body of factual and statistical information, is not an academic study. Rather, it is an attempt to find patterns and meaning emerging from a collective examination of key decisions over the past decade, complex processes in which discussants participated from different vantage points. Two areas, Senate confirmation of presidential appointments and the role of the press in congressional-executive relations, are not covered in the study, and are worthy of systematic inquiry in the future.

I believe the study's findings were reinforced just one week after the discussion group's last meeting when the Senate refused to give its advice and consent to ratification of the Comprehensive Test Ban Treaty. None of the ingredients for a successful outcome—presidential leadership, early and ongoing consultation between the branches, leadership motivated by international rather than partisan considerations, or careful congressional examination of a complex issue—were present. The process clearly broke down when more than 60 members of the Senate urged delay to avoid damage to U.S. international leadership, and yet the vote proceeded.

Relations between the executive and legislative branches of government over the direction and content of U.S. foreign policy are often marked by partisanship, dispute, deadlock, and ill-feeling. Some disagreement, of course, is inevitable in our system of constitutionally shared power, especially at a time of politically divided government with Democrats controlling the White House and Republicans controlling both houses of Congress. But it remains desirable that executive-legislative relations be conducted in a way that enhances the U.S. ability to advance its interests internationally. It is the Institute's hope that this report can make a contribution to that end.

We are grateful to the Smith Richardson Foundation, the HCS Foundation, The Otto M. Budig Family Foundation, and ISD board member L. Thomas Hiltz and his family for providing the financial support that made this project and publication possible.

CASIMIR A. YOST
Director, Institute for the Study of Diplomacy
Chair, Congress & Foreign Policy Discussion Group

1
Findings and Lessons for the Future

FINDINGS

The foreign policy struggle between the Congress and the President did not begin in the 1990s, but the past decade has been a time of substantial friction between the legislative and executive branches of government over the conduct of U.S. foreign policy. Four reasons for this friction—some old, some new—emerged clearly in this project's studies and discussions.

Shared responsibilities in foreign policy. The 1990s frictions came on top of the age-old congressional-executive struggle over U.S. foreign policy that the Constitution invites and our democratic system of government ensures.

Divided government. For much of the decade, the two branches of government were controlled by different parties.

Decline in priority. Foreign policy in the post-Cold War era has not been a high priority for the American people, nor, as a consequence, for most Members of Congress. Beginning his first term, President Clinton viewed domestic and economic concerns as the first priorities of his presidency.

Increasing complexity. The foreign policy-making process has become more complex, with proliferating executive and legislative branch participants as well as nongovernmental actors. The issues themselves often include a complex mix of foreign and domestic factors.

Legislative/executive foreign policy relationships in the 1990s have been set in a period of dramatic turnover in congressional membership. A generational revolution in executive and legislative officials

2 Findings and Lessons for the Future

brought new leaders to the fore—a process whose impact may be as important as the profound international changes produced by the end of the Cold War. Fifty members of the Senate and 353 Members of the House have been newly elected in the 1990s. These Members inevitably have different life experiences from their predecessors. Most have never fought in a war. Most have never served in the military. Only a few have had direct international experience in their previous professional lives. Virtually all are more burdened than their predecessors by the time demands placed on them by the need to raise money for increasingly expensive reelection campaigns.

The project's discussion group reflected on the difficult congressional-executive foreign policy battles of the 1970s and 1980s over Vietnam, arms control policy, relations with the Soviet Union, and aid to the Nicaragua Contra rebels. Recognizing the "permanent" nature of the conflict between the two branches, we looked for factors that made the struggles of the 1990s different, and those that could influence U.S. foreign policy-making in the years ahead.

A careful review of the cases we examined produced the following findings:

Leadership

The most decisive factor in the legislative/executive relationship on foreign policy in the 1990s was leadership. Time and time again the discussion group came back to executive branch leadership as the vital ingredient to success. Its absence was equally decisive in failure. Of the ten cases surveyed, only a few benefited from effective presidential leadership. On the congressional side, bipartisan coalition-building and internationally attuned leadership were demonstrated rarely and by too few Members.

Intraparty divisions and partisanship

Divisions within parties on foreign affairs issues are now as prominent as divisions between parties. Partisanship was frequently a factor in the foreign policy debates of the 1990s, but it was not necessarily decisive in many outcomes. Every successful executive-legislative collaboration that this group studied benefited from bipartisan support.

Mutual mistrust

One factor that strongly influenced the mood, if not the outcomes, of executive-legislative relations on foreign policy was the deep mutual mistrust between the White House and congressional Republicans. It was notable, however, that the Republican leadership in the Congress and the President managed to cooperate on several important foreign policy initiatives despite a profoundly antagonistic relationship.

Interest groups and public opinion

Interest group lobbying on a number of issues played a role but was not decisive in outcomes. Exceptions include abortion lobbies that effectively held up an agreement on UN dues,* labor interests that helped defeat fast-track legislation, and agricultural and business lobbying on lifting trade sanctions on India and Pakistan. Public opinion appears to have had a relatively small impact on congressional consideration of foreign policy issues in the 1990s.

Deteriorating congressional capacity

The congressional capacity to address foreign policy issues and constructively engage in its formulation continues to deteriorate. Specifically, the foreign affairs authorizing committees have lost much of their stature and influence. This is not a new phenomenon—its roots go back to the 1970s. But the consequences of this trend for U.S. foreign policy are troubling. The understanding, expertise, and leadership that the authorizing committees can bring to the legislative process have increasingly taken second place to the more narrow fiscal focus of the budget appropriating committees. Only three of the ten cases reviewed benefited from substantial authorization committee input.

Diffused consideration, concentrated power

Consideration of foreign affairs in the Congress has become increasingly diffused while decision-making power, especially on resource

---

*Six weeks after the project finished, the Congress approved funding for UN dues, with conditions.

issues, has become concentrated in the appropriations committees and the leadership.

New pressures on the system

Changes in the political culture of the 1990s are adding stress to the process. The "CNN factor" requires instant reactions from political figures to breaking world events, cementing positions that might be more nuanced given time for deliberation. Fund-raising for increasingly expensive campaigns is burdening already tight congressional schedules and leaving less time for in-depth inquiries into complex world issues. Time spent on foreign affairs does not yield the campaign contributions that are stimulated by work on such domestic issues as banking reform or telecommunications regulation. Attracting neither money nor votes, spending time on foreign affairs concerns is increasingly seen as a political liability.

Congress avoids responsibility on use of force issues

In Haiti, Iraq, Bosnia, and Kosovo, Members of Congress have strongly criticized presidential decisions, but the Congress has avoided either supporting the President's actions or cutting off funds to force an end to the operations. In the international environment of the 1990s, the Congress has let the President take responsibility for decisions to use force in support of U.S. national security objectives. As long as the Congress chooses neither to endorse nor block such presidential decisions, presidents will likely use the largely free hand that they are given.

Republicans more supportive of President on foreign trade

On trade issues, Republicans have generally been more supportive of presidential efforts to liberalize trade than have Democrats.

Legislative-executive collaboration on sanctions

The Congress is commonly seen as the main advocate of economic and military sales sanctions as a foreign policy tool, but the fact is that the legislative and executive branches have often collaborated on the implementation of sanctions despite serious questions about their efficacy.

Widely divergent views on China

In the case of U.S. policy toward China, both Democrats and Republicans were critical of presidential initiatives, albeit for different reasons. The vast number and complexity of the issues involved, and the strategic imperative that the United States manage the relationship successfully have led to widely diverging and strongly held views in the Congress.

Reduced resources for U.S. foreign policy

Budgetary considerations have prevailed over policy and program needs as the basis for decisions during this decade. The Congress, including both Democrats and Republicans, continues to cut funding from levels requested by an executive branch that submits bare-bones budgets. The downward budgetary pressure on discretionary spending has been a decisive factor in putting financing for U.S. foreign affairs accounts at risk.

LESSONS

The next decade is likely to be as challenging as the last. In an ideal world, diverse and conflicting views on U.S. interests would be addressed by a legislative branch attuned and attentive to the trade-offs that have to be made to achieve continued peace and prosperity for the nation. The legislative branch would be an equal partner with the executive, filling in gaps, tempering decisions, and providing early advice in times of crisis. Such a vision may be ambitious, but it nonetheless should be the standard against which the role of the Congress in foreign policy is judged.

Each of the issues the discussion group examined will be with us in the next century. Debates over resources for foreign affairs are likely to be a central feature of executive and legislative relations in the future. Decisions on how to allocate limited discretionary funds will produce splits within and between parties. Questions concerning

6 Findings and Lessons for the Future

the circumstances under which U.S. military forces should be put in harm's way will remain controversial in the Congress and between the Congress and future administrations. Indeed, congressional and executive branch leaders will likely debate whether or not current U.S. reluctance to place its forces at risk is dangerously limiting the U.S. ability to pursue its interests internationally. Unexpected developments will challenge the two branches to react effectively.

In these circumstances, how can the executive-legislative link in our foreign policy decision-making system be strengthened so that it will be up to the task? This project attempted to identify some lessons learned from the experience of the 1990s, hoping to produce useful suggestions for the next President and the Congress. What follows are general observations and specific suggestions for the future.

As consensus becomes more difficult, the need for effective dialogue increases

The most important new feature of the international system in the 1990s—the absence of any defining enemy to help shape a U.S. foreign policy consensus—seems likely to continue, at least for the next decade, if not longer. This suggests that the President and congressional leaders will have to work harder, know more, and communicate better to produce the kind of bipartisan consensus on which a strong and effective U.S. foreign policy can be based. Working together, the two branches should take every possible step to ensure that poor communication does not undermine a constructive congressional-executive dialogue on foreign policy issues even when there may be serious disagreements about policy directions.

Presidential leadership will remain the most important requirement

The Congress, like much of the world, looks to the President of the United States for effective leadership. The President must frame issues, develop initiatives, and actively engage the Congress in the process of making U.S. foreign policy.

- Executive branch foreign policy officials should spend more time, energy, and resources consulting with Members of Congress and their staff to lower the level of executive-legislative distrust and increase Member participation in foreign policy formulation. Consultation should be an ongoing dialogue, with as much informal give-and-take as formal and structured briefings and testimony. The President should lead this effort with vigor and personal commitment.

- In choosing the administration's foreign policy team, the President should ensure that foreign policy nominees are strongly committed to the goal of establishing effective congressional-executive foreign policy working relationships.

- Legislative affairs bureaus in executive branch agencies should be bridges rather than barriers to communication between the two branches. The next administration should enlist a bipartisan group of prominent individuals to participate in strengthening the legislative affairs operations at the Department of State, the Department of Defense, and the National Security Council. The Congress should invite the State Department to establish a liaison office on the Hill to facilitate an ongoing dialogue with Members and committees.

Congress must become a better partner in the foreign policy process

The Congress also has leadership responsibilities. Even though Members of Congress are elected to represent districts or states, congressional leadership is most effective when it is primarily influenced by the same standards of statesmanship and national interest that are used to judge the President's performance. The system does not work well unless congressional leaders, including the Speaker of the House, the Minority Leader, the Majority and Minority Leaders in the Senate, and the chairmen of key committees base their actions on interpretations of national interest rather than partisan or regional agendas.

The Congress should once again address the issue of its capacity to be a partner in the making of foreign policy. It did so in the 1970s, and the new international circumstances that have accompanied the end of the Cold War justify another serious self-examination.

The Congress should establish a bipartisan, bicameral commission to study the role of the Congress in foreign policy. Such a commission should examine ways in which the Congress might improve

8 Findings and Lessons for the Future

its ability to handle its foreign policy responsibilities, including the following:

- The diminished influence of the foreign policy authorizing committees seriously undermines the role of the Congress in foreign policy formulation. Congressional leaders should adopt a long-term strategy to revitalize the Senate Foreign Relations and the House International Relations committees as important players in the shaping of U.S. foreign policy. As part of this effort, members should explore ways to distribute power more evenly between authorizers and appropriators through ex-officio mutual membership on relevant subcommittees, formal or informal caucusing, or other techniques.

- The congressional seniority culture should be replaced by an interest and ability culture. The congressional party caucuses should commit themselves to identifying Members who are knowledgeable about and interested in foreign affairs to fill leadership positions in foreign affairs. They should select "team building" rather than "agenda setting" Members for such positions. To facilitate a process of change, the Republican House decision to rotate chairs of committees should be adopted by both parties and both houses. The intraparty harmony brought about by adherence to a seniority system is less important to the nation than an effective congressional role in foreign policy.

- The Appropriations committees should realign subcommittee jurisdictions to separate the State Department from the Justice and Commerce Departments. The reorganized State Department has new responsibilities, is facing increased security threats to American embassies, and is pursuing a unique representational mission overseas. It should receive attentive budget oversight that is not, at the subcommittee level, competing with domestic agencies for congressional time or funding.

- Both Houses should form permanent bipartisan national security observer groups consisting of the chairs and ranking members of the key committees and leadership posts. The groups should be modeled after the Arms Control and NATO Observer Groups that have proven their value in helping prepare the

Congress to make informed decisions on foreign policy issues in the past. Such groups would have neither legislative nor oversight mandates. They would not eclipse committees any more than the National Security Council in the executive branch takes the place of the State or Defense Departments. Their function would be to facilitate early and ongoing consultation between the two branches and to nurture congressional expertise on vital security issues.

- Both houses should explore new ways of breaking through impasses and allowing majorities to prevail on important national issues. Legislative means should be found and used to break away single issues from larger legislative vehicles. Single-Member holds on nominees should be abolished in the Senate.

- Members should make full use of the expert and independent resources at their command, including more extensive use of staff members from the Congressional Research Service, the General Accounting Office, and the Congressional Budget Office. The Congressional Research Service should be directed to rebuild its contingent of foreign and security policy senior specialists whose ranks have been decimated by retirements and transfers and the fact that no new senior specialists have been appointed in the 1990s.

- As one way to improve congressional-executive foreign policy ties, the current programs that place executive branch foreign and defense policy officials in congressional offices as "fellows" should be expanded. The administration should establish an orientation program designed to introduce new committee and Member staff with foreign policy responsibilities to executive branch foreign policy offices and agencies.

- The American people should expect their foreign policy decisionmakers, including Members of Congress, to have first-hand knowledge of facts and perspectives that can be gained through purposeful foreign travel. The executive branch, press, and public should encourage Members to travel abroad as part of official delegations and for parliamentary exchanges. Opportunities to build credibility with foreign counterparts and pursue fact-finding missions contribute directly to the ability of the Congress to participate constructively in the U.S. foreign policy-making process. The Congress must penalize "boondoggle" abuses of travel while supporting serious efforts to enhance the congressional role in foreign policy.

Congress and the President must reengage the American people

Legislators and executive branch officials alike have the responsibility to engage the electorate in decisions that will influence the future well-being of the nation. The U.S. role in the twenty-first century must match the resources of the nation and the will of its people. An intensified dialogue between national leaders and the American people on issues like resources for foreign affairs and the use of force should seek to close the current gap between views of the electorate and the way they are perceived by leaders in Washington.

2
Congress and Foreign Policy in the 1990s

THE PAST IS PROLOGUE

Over the last decade—since the end of the Cold War—the Congress and the President have sometimes cooperated but too often have struggled unsuccessfully to reach a consensus on U.S. foreign policy purposes and means. Some of the differences have been based on dissimilar substantive and institutional priorities; some have had profoundly partisan roots; and others have grown out of personal factors influencing relationships between the current President and the Congress.

Legislative-executive interaction on foreign policy is deeply rooted in the structure of the relationship between the Congress and the President established in the Constitution. Professor E.S. Corwin's observation that the Constitution provides an "invitation to struggle for the privilege of directing American foreign policy" is on the mark. Shared and overlapping responsibility for shaping and implementing U.S. foreign policy ensures that there will be tensions and conflicts between the two branches. But other factors are at work as well.

The war in Vietnam was a contemporary turning point. As Professor James Lindsay wrote in 1992, after Vietnam, "[t]he deference Congress once accorded the president gave way to active questioning of presidential initiatives. Bipartisanship vanished . . . and the inside game, where a handful of senior legislators spoke for Congress on major issues, gave way to an outside game, where many legislators influenced policy."

The divisions between the Congress and the President over Vietnam were far more serious and disruptive than anything seen since. U.S. involvement in Vietnam still constitutes the most contentious "use-of-force" issue in the second half of the twentieth century, and its profound influence on presidential and congressional perceptions persists today.

The Senate's constitutional role in the treaty-making process often has provided the ground on which Presidents and the Congress have both contested foreign policy goals and methods and collaborated to advance U.S. interests. Remembering how the Senate blocked U.S. participation in the League of Nations following the First World War, the administration of President Harry Truman in the late 1940s recognized the importance of bringing the Congress along in pursuing such important post-war initiatives as the North Atlantic Treaty, the United Nations, and Marshall Plan aid to Europe. Throughout the post-World War II period, Members have nonetheless remained concerned about the quality of consultations and collaboration that successive Presidents have offered the Congress on important foreign policy issues.

The 1970s and 1980s produced passionate and partisan debate on a number of foreign policy issues in addition to Vietnam. Divisions over policy toward the Soviet Union were reflected in debates about strategic arms control treaties negotiated with Moscow. The Soviet invasion of Afghanistan in 1979 provided grounds for Members of Congress to question the Carter administration's conduct of détente policies with the Russians. And in the late 1970s, some congressional Republicans criticized President Carter for "giving away" the Panama Canal.

In the 1980s, when Republican President Ronald Reagan took a hard line toward Moscow, congressional Democrats suggested that the President was leading relations with the Soviet Union toward an intensified Cold War. Aid to the contra rebels in Nicaragua in the 1980s, with the goal of overthrowing Nicaragua's leftist Sandinista government, provoked strong differences between President Reagan and congressional Democrats. When the Congress limited funding for such support, the Reagan administration sought clandestine ways to get assistance to the rebels.

The Congress has historically exercised its constitutionally given power of the purse to influence policy choices. Congressional-executive differences over how much to spend on the conduct of U.S. foreign policy and what levels of foreign aid are most appropriate have been a persistent feature of the U.S. foreign policy debate since the

Second World War. Foreign aid and the State Department were not much more popular with Members of Congress in the 1970s and 1980s than they have been in the 1990s.

This said, just as Vietnam may be regarded as an important watershed in congressional-executive relations on foreign policy, the end of the Cold War can be seen as a fundamental change in international relations that also affected the role of the Congress in foreign policy.

A NEW ERA FOR FOREIGN POLICY-MAKING

The end of the Cold War removed a bipartisan touchstone for congressional analysis of fast-paced and complex developments overseas. The need for systematic inquiries, sustained congressional oversight, and a balanced overview of how to pursue U.S. interests in the world has grown at a time when Members' attention to foreign affairs issues has diminished and fragmented.

Through the mid-1990s, the U.S. budget deficit and the political consensus on behalf of eliminating that deficit became an important standard by which U.S. foreign policy commitments and resources were judged. Republicans and Democrats, the Congress and the administration agreed that the deficit was a challenge to U.S. security even if they were not always able to agree on how to deal with this threat.

Defense spending was less affected by concerns about the budget deficit. Congressional Republicans were largely united on preserving current levels or even increasing defense outlays. President Clinton and most congressional Democrats, on the other hand, did not want to be perceived as weak on defense issues and did not seek substantial cuts in defense spending. There was no such consensus, however, on the resources that should be provided for the conduct of U.S. foreign relations or on questions concerning the use of U.S. forces in peace operations overseas.

In fact, the shift of focus—from Cold War requirements to the discipline of deficit reduction—appears to have influenced the way in which the Congress participated in the foreign policy process. The new circumstances placed a higher priority on the role of the appropriations process, where spending trade-offs are shaped and managed. Post-Cold War priorities deemphasized the importance of the authorizing committees, where foreign policy oversight is ideally conducted and the informational basis for congressional action is developed. As a consequence, fundamental decisions about U.S. foreign policy were increasingly shaped by resource availability and allocation, a "focus on purse over policy," as one ISD discussion member put it. This shift enhanced the role of the House and Senate appropriations committees and reduced the role of the House Foreign Affairs/International Relations* and the Senate Foreign Relations committees.

The decline of the foreign affairs authorizing committees has continued through the 1990s. In fact, authorizing committees played a key role in only three of the ten cases the discussion group examined (State Department reorganization, UN funding, and NATO enlargement). The decline has diminished the base of congressional foreign affairs expertise independent of the executive branch and has stymied leadership development and earlier consensus on divisive issues.

The decline in the quality of attention paid to foreign policy issues, observed over the last decade, has many roots. The end of the Cold War changed the context by removing the threat that had helped forge compromise and even consensus in the past. In this new environment, important domestic and financial issues became the main preoccupation of the President and the Congress. Further, Republican control of the House and generational change in both chambers during the decade have placed new legislators, less experienced in foreign affairs, in positions of responsibility, at least temporarily weakening the system's capability to function effectively and produce good policy. To illustrate the point, during the 105th Congress, first-term Senators chaired all the Senate Foreign Relations subcommittees. And, in both houses, the leadership has made many critical decisions without necessarily benefiting from deliberations and advice from the authorizing committees.

The increased mingling of foreign and domestic policies issues and the reform of the congressional establishment have contributed

---

*The House Committee on International Relations was called the "Committee on Foreign Affairs" until 1975 and from 1979 until 1995. From 1975 to 1979 it was called the "Committee on International Relations," its current designation.

to a diffusion of power in the Congress. One former administration official in the ISD discussion group commented that "power is fragmented on the Hill" and noted that the problem of congressional leadership became worse when, "in 1994, people took leadership who had never had to lead." Another discussion group member with experience in both branches agreed, noting that ". . . there is a distinct impression of a diffusion of power. The luxury of being able to reach an agreement with a small number of leaders has given way to the need to negotiate case by case and issue by issue with individual members who have their own agendas."

Almost every committee is seized with one or more issues having foreign policy implications. The number of players has increased, old coalitions of internationalists have broken up, and leadership on foreign policy issues is coming from unexpected places. For example, the Agriculture Committees held hearings on funding for the International Monetary Fund (IMF). Congressman Chris Cox chaired a select committee on China that has set the tone in the House for consideration of U.S.-China issues. And the Government Affairs committees on both sides of the Capitol play active roles in nuclear nonproliferation and international narcotics trafficking issues.

The House International Relations Committee and the Senate Foreign Relations Committee never had a monopoly on foreign policy, but their chairmen and Members were seen as resident experts, and their voices were listened to and often heeded. Now very few are regarded as experts, and many voices seem more or less equal. Meanwhile, party leaders find it more difficult to shape a working consensus. As one senior Senate staffer commented, "A critical factor contributing to the messiness is the erosion of party discipline. It began in the Seventies, but it is now more difficult to rally the troops and gather the votes."

The role of the State Department as the lead executive branch agency for foreign policy has been undermined by comparable factors within the executive branch. Other agencies have taken the lead on major foreign policy issues, effectively diminishing State's authority. Some discussion group members were highly critical of the State Department's Legislative Affairs Bureau. A former high-level Clinton Administration official observed that, with regard to one of the cases studied ". . . the State Department was constipated as usual by the desire of the Legislative Affairs Bureau to control all contacts with Congress and to control all access to the Secretary about congressional matters." Another discussant argued that Legislative Affairs needs to think of itself more as a bridge than a dam to communications. "The whole idea of having such a bureau is to put a little oversight and control into the process of relations with the Hill," argued one participant, defending the purpose if not the execution of the effort. Although many in the group sympathized with the need for the administration to "speak with one voice" to the Congress, the consensus was for more open, frequent, and ongoing communication between State Department officials and the Hill.

Relations between the executive and legislative branches during this decade have been an uneasy mix of tolerance, distrust, and, on some significant occasions, collaboration. The Congress ultimately has supported, or has not blocked, major Bush and Clinton administration foreign policy initiatives with regard to the Gulf War, the North American Free Trade Agreement (NAFTA), the General Agreement on Tariffs and Trade (GATT), U.S. peacekeeping troops in Bosnia and Kosovo, and NATO enlargement. The Congress supported IMF funding after a healthy debate on the role of the institution and the future of the international financial system. The Congress has continued to support the deployment of one hundred thousand U.S. troops forward-deployed both in Asia and in Europe.

Congressional leaders have taken initiatives to fill some perceived vacuums. For example, Senators Nunn and Lugar formulated an aid program to Russia to reduce the threat of "loose nukes" that is now an important component of U.S.-Russian relations. Senator Helms pursued reorganization of the foreign affairs agencies after similar executive branch proposals became mired in bureaucratic gridlock.

Seeking to enhance its influence on U.S. foreign policy, the Congress has been energetic in passing economic sanctions against other countries—frequently despite executive branch objections, albeit more often than not acceded to and occasionally led by the President. The United States, according to one count, has imposed economic sanctions 104 times since World War II, sixty-one of these since President Clinton assumed office. This resort to sanctions has been interpreted at home and abroad as a preference for pursuing unilateral American foreign policies rather than cooperative or multilateral approaches. The Helms-Burton sanctions legislation, intended to punish corporations for doing business with Cuba, is often cited as an example of the tendency of the Congress to rely heavily on sanctions. Of course, such legislation cannot be enacted without the President's signature. With his right to waive the sanctions, the actual impact has probably been more symbolic than substantial.

Without doubt, differences between the two government branches have also resulted in deadlock. The foreign policy ledger contains consequent failures that will continue to damage U.S. interests. The Congress did not approve "fast-track" trade negotiating authority for the President, thwarting a longtime U.S. leadership role in pursuing free trade. The President and the Congress took several years trying to find a way to pay UN arrears, overdue by more than $1 billion. By flouting its obligations, the United States hindered UN reform, diminished its influence in the institution, and undermined its authority around the world in asking other nations to live up to their international obligations. The foreign affairs budget is another area of woeful performance. It has continued to decline, with blame to be shared by both branches, despite efforts by some key individuals to turn the tide. The decline comes at a time when diplomacy has become more complicated and U.S. interests more numerous and difficult to pursue.

Throughout the 1990s, the predisposition of the Congress to question the judgment and candor of the executive branch appears to have grown. Putting this factor in historical perspective, one study group participant with extensive executive branch experience suggested that "[t]he mistrust between the executive and the legislative branches is hard to get past. There has been a lack of candor on the part of the executive, whether in Vietnam, Iran-Contra, Central America, or other cases where the administration [in office] has not been honest or concealed facts." Such mistrust inevitably feeds the fires of partisanship, and partisan behavior in the 1990s has been aggravated by the view of President Clinton held by many congressional Republicans. As one experienced Hill observer noted, "The personal factor that Bill Clinton introduces into the equation is unique. Suspicion of him as a human being is not just partisanship in the way that a Democratic Congress looked with a fishy eye at George Bush." The general congressional distrust of the executive branch, combined with the Clinton factor, has made it more difficult to develop consensual, bipartisan approaches to foreign policy issues.

In addition, a variety of "new" issues have intruded on foreign policy decisions, including economic, environmental, and social concerns. The contemporary security environment, which appears to many Americans as less threatening, is hardly free from peril. Rogue states or individual terrorist groups armed with nuclear devices or biological and chemical weapons may be on the near horizon. The United States and China could find each other facing off over Taiwan. The Asian financial crisis, and ensuing political instability, may have been just a warning of worse crises to come. Russia, which still has thousands of deliverable nuclear weapons, continues to face political and economic weaknesses that pose unique challenges to stability. Meanwhile, domestic political, social and economic issues mix more liberally with international policy, forcing policymakers to address more and more foreign policy questions with reference to a combination of international and domestic factors.

A substantial challenge lies ahead. Most would agree that U.S. interests are ultimately best served by a national foreign policy consensus representing the collective judgment of both the legislative and executive branches of government. One good measure of success, according to one ISD discussion participant, is "whether policies proceed from a truly intelligent debate about the policies and their implications." How can the prospects for such an outcome be enhanced as we enter the twenty-first century? What is necessary to foster in the Congress and the Executive Branch a more constructive, consensual foreign policy and closer collaboration on its implementation?

3
Key Factors

Most of the ten foreign policy issues from the past decade that the ISD discussion group reviewed not only have links to the past but also are likely to confront Presidents and the Congress in the twenty-first century. The cases were chosen because they entailed significant interaction between the administration and the Congress in the 1990s, had historical roots in the Cold War period, and involved issues that would likely be faced by the Congress and the President in the future. The lessons from these cases therefore are not only of historical significance: they may also help the next President and the Congress develop more effective U.S. foreign policy approaches. (The cases themselves are outlined in some detail in the next chapter.)

LEADERSHIP

In every case study, the quality of presidential and congressional leadership was a key factor determining how well or how poorly the system worked. Over the past decade, the record has been mixed. But, on balance, neither the President nor the Congress received high marks for consistent leadership from our discussion group.

Most of the cases studied involved the interaction between the Clinton presidency and the Congress. One, however, focused primarily on the Bush administration. Senators Nunn and Lugar's initiative to provide assistance to the former Soviet Union to ensure the safety of nuclear weapons and technology came at a time when President Bush, otherwise known as strongly committed to foreign policy leadership, was trying to strengthen perceptions of his competence on

THE TEN CASES

1. **Nunn-Lugar and Soviet weapons of mass destruction**—a congressional initiative designed to deal with the possibility that weapons of mass destruction could "leak" out of a disintegrating Soviet Union;

2. **Bosnia, Kosovo, and the use of force**—the role of the Congress concerning the use of U.S. military forces in recent Balkan crises;

3. **NATO enlargement**—the issue of whether or not to bring new Central and East European democracies into the North Atlantic Treaty Organization.

4. **U.S. policy toward China**—interaction between the President and the Congress concerning how to deal with a wide variety of issues and interests in the U.S.-China relationship;

5. **Fast-track trade negotiating authority**—the question of giving the President authority to negotiate trade deals that cannot be amended by the Congress and must be voted up or down in a given time period;

6. **Increasing the International Monetary Fund quota**—the issue of increasing the funds the United States allocates for loans made by the IMF to promote international financial stability and growth;

7. **Resources for foreign affairs**—the issue of how much money is required to fund U.S. foreign policy agencies and the tools of U.S. foreign policy, including foreign aid and public diplomacy;

8. **State Department reorganization**—the effort to merge the U.S. Information Agency, the Arms Control and Disarmament Agency, and the Agency for International Development into the State Department;

9. **Glenn Amendment of 1994**—the issue of how to use sanctions to try to deter India and Pakistan from detonating nuclear weapons;

10. **Funding for the United Nations**—the question of whether and under what conditions the United States should pay the full amount of arrears owed the UN.

domestic policy. In spite of the administration's perceived strengths in foreign and defense policy, President Bush and his advisors did not devote high priority to this issue until Senators Nunn and Lugar had taken the lead.

President Clinton's foreign policy leadership in his relationship with the Congress was a central topic of discussion. His is a ledger listing both successes and defeats. As one participant noted, "The interesting thing is how even in a space of two years in the same administration you can have such different outcomes." The North American Free Trade Agreement, a case the group did not examine, and the expansion of NATO and funding for the IMF are clearly on the plus side of the President's ledger. But, on balance, the Clinton presidency received relatively low marks from the ISD discussion group for leading the executive-congressional interaction on foreign policy.

The administration's approach to gaining congressional support for its policy toward the Bosnia crisis was viewed as inadequate, with administration witnesses first telling the Congress that the conflict in the Balkans did not affect vital U.S. interests, then vacillating on lifting the arms embargo and failing to consult sufficiently with the Congress to build support for its ultimate decision to deploy U.S. troops there. With regard to fast-track trade negotiating authority, the President was unable to win over enough Democrats in 1997 to obtain passage of the necessary legislation. One member of the study group observed that "the Senate will always be more protectionist than the President, and the House will always be more protectionist than the Senate. . . . If the President isn't 110 percent committed, [fast track] just can't happen."

Regarding the issue of UN funding, the White House was for years unable to make the effort required to resolve the issue. Along the way, the issue was linked by Senate Foreign Relations Chairman Jesse Helms to his goal of merging the U.S. Information Agency and the Arms Control and Disarmament Agency with the Department of State. The administration accepted the consolidation concept but was not able to de-link UN funding from House Republican-sponsored antiabortion provisions, which then led to a presidential veto of the package. Reorganization was then accomplished through the Omnibus Appropriation Bill. The discussion group also judged that President Clinton had never taken personal interest in the goal of building congressional support for the administration's policy of "active engagement" with China and that neither Presidents Bush nor Clinton

22 Key Factors

Congressional Support of the President:
Percentage votes on both foreign and domestic issues

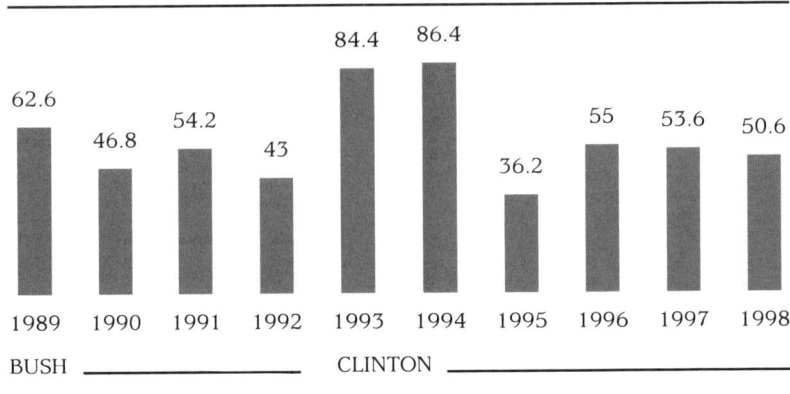

Source: *Congressional Quarterly Almanac*, 1998.

had provided sufficient leadership on behalf of the overall foreign affairs budget.

On the positive side of the ledger, the executive branch's successful effort on IMF funding was led by Secretary of the Treasury Robert Rubin and, subsequently, White House Chief of Staff Erskine Bowles, who did a decisive job of making the President's case. President Clinton was seen as having provided essential leadership on the issue of NATO enlargement, particularly in getting the process started in 1994. The President and other administration officials worked closely with congressional leaders, particularly through the newly created Senate NATO Observer Group, in the year before the Senate vote to build a strong bipartisan coalition in the Congress. This kept the initiative on track and produced a successful outcome for administration policy.

Discussion group members felt that the President was effective in lobbying for administration foreign policy goals when he made the effort. However, all too often he was distracted by other demands and priorities and only rarely engaged in long-term consultation and consensus building.

The discussion group also examined congressional leadership in foreign affairs. The Congress represents the diverse views and conflicting interests of the American people and is not institutionally designed to take the lead on foreign policy. But the Congress has important constitutional responsibilities.

Congressional Support of the President:
Votes on defense and foreign policy issues

1989   President Bush prevailed:
         79 percent of the time in the Senate
         58 percent in the House

1998   President Clinton prevailed:
         75 percent of the time in the Senate
         13 percent in the House

Source: *Congressional Quarterly Almanac,* 1998.

Individual Members, particularly those in leadership positions or those who have developed acknowledged and respected expertise, can provide significant leadership that determines outcome. But the record of the 1990s is mixed. As one academic member of the discussion group observed, "Members of Congress don't want to lead for fear of being held responsible. . . . They don't want to lead unless the outcome is safe." Another discussant expressed a pessimistic appraisal, "The system has been able to go around a weak person in one position or another but the difference now is that there is a lack of effective and committed leaders in almost all the key positions." Other participants argued that the case studies belie such a negative assessment. Leaders did emerge, sometimes at the last minute and sometimes from unexpected quarters. On balance, however, despite moments of triumph by individual Members on some key issues, most participants agreed that congressional leadership in foreign affairs lacks a sense of overall purpose and commitment to sustained inquiry.

The group was especially critical of the congressional approach to the commitment of U.S. forces overseas. Members of Congress are highly vocal in questioning or reproaching the President when he makes decisions to use force, but the institution has been unwilling to take responsibility for either approving or blocking the President's initiatives. The main focus of the group's discussion was on the decision to send troops to enforce the peace in Bosnia, but the tendencies exhibited in that debate seemed more generally applicable. A majority of Members of the House and Senate opposed the original commitment, particularly when it appeared that U.S. forces might suffer significant casualties. However, as the operation proceeded successfully, opposition to the mission diminished.

24 Key Factors

Political Divisions in the Congress

	Senate		House	
	Democrats	Republicans	Democrats	Republicans
102nd (1991–92)	55	45	260	175
106th* (1999–00)	45	55	211	221

*As of June 1999, 1 independent.
Source: Thomas online.

The Congress has not asserted its constitutionally based powers for declaring war, limiting itself to reviewing the cost of U.S. operational deployments in Bosnia and elsewhere and using the power of the purse to insist on conditions that it wants the administration to impose on such commitments. The question may be whether this approach, driven more by resource issues and emotional "support the troops" arguments than by policy and national interest considerations, is adequate when decisions are being made to put American soldiers in harm's way. Some members of the discussion group also felt that, with regard to use of force issues, President Clinton had continued, and even intensified, the recent presidential practice of effectively marginalizing the role of the Congress in decisions that get the United States into conflict situations.

Of course, some cases did reveal congressional leadership. For example, during the IMF debate, congressional leadership overcame party splits while addressing serious doubts about the IMF's ability to help stabilize the ongoing international financial crises in Asia and Russia. Speaker Newt Gingrich, along with Representative Bob Livingston, was able to help resolve the issue in the face of opposition from other members of the House leadership. Minority Leader Gephardt also played a constructive role in dealing with environmental and social issue concerns in his own party. Congressman Jim Leach organized extensive hearings in the Banking Committee, and authorizing legislation was voted out 40–9, although the issue was never given an up or down vote in the House. On the Senate side, Senator Gramm played both a public and a behind-the-scenes role. Senator Chuck

Number of Incoming Freshmen

Election Year	Senate	House
1990	5	43
1992	14	110
1994	11	86
1996	15	74
1998	5	40
Total	50	353

Source: *Congressional Quarterly* almanacs, 1990–1996 and *Congressional Quarterly Weekly*, November 7, 1998.

Average Age of Members of Congress

	All	Senate	House
102nd	53.6	57.2	52.8
103rd	52.9	58.0	51.7
104th	52.2	58.4	50.9
105th	52.7	57.5	51.6
106th	53.7	58.3	52.6

Source: *Congressional Quarterly Weekly*, January 9, 1999.

Hagel worked closely with Senator Mitch McConnell on certification requirements that were essential to the vote of 84–16 in the Senate. Senator Stevens pushed for a resolution of the issue despite doubts of his own. Without such congressional leadership, the issue could have languished unresolved indefinitely.

Other issues where leadership stood out included the Nunn-Lugar legislation. The two senators worked through the party caucuses in introducing and pursuing their proposal. They defined it as a form of self-defense. Senators Biden and Helms provided leadership on UN funding, each for his own reasons. Senator Biden felt obliged because of his role as minority leader on the Senate Foreign Relations Committee and Senator Helms because he wanted to prevail on the substantively unrelated but politically linked issue of State Department reorganization. The UN funding approach failed at the last minute when it became linked to the abortion issue. The leadership in the House can be criticized for not convincing members to de-link the issues so that UN funding could move forward.

Finally, one important foreign policy issue, NATO enlargement, received impressive bipartisan congressional leadership. Early Republican support was demonstrated in the 1994 "Contract With America" list of campaign pledges. In subsequent years, close cooperation behind the scenes between administration officials and staff for Republicans and Democrats in the Senate helped produce eighty votes in favor, comfortably beyond the required two-thirds majority.

In brief, there is a continuing need for foreign policy leadership on the Hill as well as in the White House. Several members of the discussion group noted that the ranks of effective foreign policy leaders in the Congress are thin. One former Hill staffer remarked that "[t]here used to be strong leaders in the Senate where if Hubert Humphrey or Jacob Javits or Clifford Case went somewhere, others followed." In the same vein, a veteran Hill observed that "Members don't want responsibility. They want to futz around with the bumper sticker stuff. There are too few Bidens and Lugars and Hamiltons." Another discussant, while concerned about the quality of current congressional foreign policy leadership, had a more optimistic view of the future. "I see more people rising in the system who will treat these issues with care and meet their responsibilities in shaping America's international policy."

INTEREST GROUPS

Interest groups are not a new factor in American politics. Our representational system of government invites citizens with specific interests to organize to pursue their goals. In recent decades, for example, the Greek lobby has influenced U.S. policy toward the Mediterranean region, particularly concerning Greece's conflicted relationship with Turkey. The American Jewish community has, since the creation of Israel, been one of the most powerful foreign policy lobbies in the United States. Other national minority groups, such as those representing the Baltic nations and central and East European states, have strong Washington lobbies. Historically, organized labor, business, and agricultural interests have been effective lobbyists on foreign as well as domestic policy issues.

What is new is that powerful modern media and communication tools have expanded the ability of special interest groups to exert pressure on Members of Congress. The tried-and-true tool of mail campaigns to Members has been fortified by electronic mail that can begin arriving in a Member's office soon after an issue breaks into the headlines. Low voter turnout may also give increased influence to interest groups that represent minority perspectives on issues but can mobilize votes and contribute money, especially in primary elections.

The interaction between interest groups and the role of the Congress in U.S. foreign policy decisions influence how the United States is seen elsewhere in the world. In other nations, perceived congressional responsiveness to special interest groups is judged as one of the most offensive and difficult aspects of U.S. foreign policy. The Congress is variously perceived as an outlet for American unilateralism and isolationism, both of which are interpreted as arising from an insufficiently strategic perspective on international affairs and from special domestic interest group advocacies and pressure.

The ISD group's discussions suggested that interest groups can play an important role in shaping both presidential and congressional perspectives on foreign policy issues. In part, this is a legitimate and constitutionally intended consequence of democratic government. It is particularly true that individual Members of Congress are influenced by special interests that may or may not coincide with a broader view of national interests.

In the group's discussions of case studies, we found special interests to have played influential roles in several instances, sometimes in support of administration policy and sometimes against. For example, organized labor was instrumental in defeating "fast-track" trade negotiating authority for the President. Its position on labor standards and the environment, sometimes used as stalking horses against any moves to liberalize trade, affected the debate on both fast-track and IMF funding.

The abortion issue, raised every year in one way or another by religious-based conservative groups, delayed consideration of IMF funding and for several years defeated attempts to pay U.S. arrears to the United Nations. According to one executive branch discussion group member, "There is a coalition behind the antiabortion 'Mexico City language' of some sixty-odd House Members that are very tight and good bargainers.* They made it clear that the language would be important to them when it came time to vote for a Speaker." Another

---

*The term "Mexico City language" refers to the population policy of the Reagan and Bush administrations, enunciated at the 1984 UN population conference in Mexico City. The original policy was enacted by executive orders that President Clinton rescinded. The policy had banned the use of U.S. funds for international family planning groups that perform or advocate abortions or that lobby foreign governments on the issue. Recent proposals have attempted to reinstate and codify, with modifications, the Reagan-Bush policy.

discussion group member working for the House saw the issue as a clash between two domestically oriented interest groups. "On the UN, you had a Republican House held hostage by one outside group, the National Right to Life Committee, which was joined at the hip to Congressman Chris Smith, against a group surrounding the first lady's office led by the Population Action Council. Neither had any interest in the UN."

The antiabortion coalition came into play again when more votes were needed for fast-track authority and compromise Mexico City language was offered to the White House in exchange for fast track votes, but the White House declined. The antiabortion lobby also influenced the handling of funding for foreign affairs, otherwise known as the "Function 150" account in the federal budget. Representative Smith and other Republicans managed to tie the anti-family-planning language to the authorization legislation and push it through conference, albeit with insufficient votes to override a presidential veto.

Commercial interests, especially agriculture, were highly effective in pursuing the lifting of Glenn Amendment sanctions on India and Pakistan. Agricultural interests were described as more effective than banking and business on IMF funding as well. Commercial interests were unsuccessful on fast-track. Business groups lobbied on behalf of paying U.S. arrears to the UN, but gave higher priority to supporting IMF funding. Business interests have been instrumental in boosting political support for most-favored-nation treatment for China, and defense contractors, in particular, were active in supporting NATO enlargement. The discussion group felt in general that commercial interests had a leg up in access to Members because of campaign and other financial contributions from their Political Action Committees (PACs). But several discussion group members denied the common public perception that votes on issues are exchanged for financial support. "Campaign fund-raising is the fleecing of corporate America," remarked one former congressional staffer who now lobbies for several corporate clients. "There is almost no impact whatsoever for all the money that's put into it. If PACs dictated, there would be no sanctions."

Nongovernmental organizations played a supporting role in favor of paying U.S. arrears to the United Nations but had limited influence on the outcome. One organization, the United Nations

Association, opposed the administration's acceptance of forty-two certifications on funding contained in the failed compromise legislation.

Ethnic groups were active in supporting NATO enlargement, where Polish, Czech, and Hungarian-American groups, as well as organizations representing other Central and East European ethnic groups, lobbied long and hard. One discussant, deeply involved in the NATO debate, questioned whether the ethnic groups actually affected the outcome or whether they were simply pushing with the wind. "Scratching conventional wisdom, the ethnic groups played only a minor role," he said. "There were no electoral consequences for a senator ignoring interest group pressures on this issue." Ethnic Chinese-American coalitions have sought with only limited effect to pressure the Congress for improved U.S.-China relations, while most agree that the government of Taiwan has been more effective in representing its perspective. In addition, various national religious organizations are lobbying for greater religious freedom in China.

The fact that special interests can, and do, influence U.S. foreign policy decisions is not perverse—it is one way that the U.S. government represents the interests of its citizens. In some cases, however, the influence of interest groups appears to go beyond what is reasonable, both from a democratic perspective and in terms of what makes good foreign policy. Perhaps the most troubling cases are those in which single-issue proponents have successfully diverted the debate and outcome to serve more narrow objectives. For example, in an effort to force the President's hand regarding overseas population programs, abortion opponents defeated UN funding. On the other side, the pro-choice lobby leaned on the White House to prevent a compromise. It is a case in which an essentially domestic debate spilled over to damage the international reputation and influence of the United States.

The extent to which "single-issue" lobbies or well-funded commercial groups will continue to play a major role in the shaping of U.S. foreign policy will depend on the leeway given them by elected officials and the voters. The degree of their influence will also be regulated in part by whether or not voters are sufficiently concerned to communicate their views to the administration and the Congress through the ballot box and through direct communication with their senators and representatives.

Public Opinion
Do you approve or disapprove
of the way the Congress is doing its job?

	Approve	Disapprove	Don't know
Aug. 1988	42	53	5
Nov. 1990	24	72	4
Oct. 1991	45	50	5
Apr. 1992	17	78	5
Nov. 1993	28	66	6
Sept. 1994	24	70	5
June 1995	43	43	14
Aug. 1996	42	52	7
Oct. 1997	36	57	7
Oct. 1998	45	44	11
Dec. 1998	39	56	5
June 1999	48	46	6

Source: ABC/WP polls accessed on the Roper Index website.

PUBLIC OPINION

It is common for Members of Congress and the President to try to legitimize their positions by asserting that they are supported by a majority of Americans. In doing so they explicitly or implicitly develop an image of "the public" which, even if inaccurate, can become part of the conventional wisdom if left unchallenged.

One discussion group member, who is an expert on public opinion, reported that while congressional members and staff interviewed in one of his studies largely believed Americans have a negative view of the United Nations, polling data demonstrated that a majority of Americans support the UN, U.S. participation in it, and even favor strengthening the organization. In fact, a CNN/USA Today poll in November 1997 found 85 percent of those polled agreeing that "the United Nations play[s] a necessary role in the world today." On occasion, when Members claim that their perspective is supported by public opinion, it may be more accurate to say that their actions are

Costs of Winning Congressional Campaigns
(in millions of dollars)

	1998	1996	1994	1992	1990
Senate					
Raised	$161	$120	$146	$117	$120
Spent	155	122	144	121	112
House					
Raised	322	318	241	229	194
Spent	277	287	220	230	172

Source: Federal Election Commission website.

Voter Turnout (%)

1998	36.4
1996	49.08
1994	38.78
1992	55.09
1990	36.52

Source: Federal Election Commission website.

supported in their districts or states by the portion of the public that votes for them.

The explanation for this apparent weakness in the representative nature of the system may be the old saw that "the squeaky wheel gets the grease." The majority of Americans do not express themselves actively on most public policy issues and rank foreign policy issues low in priority. Not once in the 1990s was a foreign affairs question among the top four topics of concern to the American public, according to nationwide Gallup polls. It is one thing to respond to public opinion polls; it is entirely another to take active steps to influence policy.

During the 1990s, some observers have described Americans as going through a neo-isolationist phase in the wake of the Cold War, even though this image has been demolished repeatedly by numerous pollsters and reputable scholars. Some Members of Congress cite an isolationist public to justify their position on cutting the international affairs budget, reducing foreign aid, resisting multilateral cooperation, and holding back on UN dues.

The Republican victory in the 1994 congressional elections was interpreted by some as signaling a growing disinterest in U.S. involvement overseas. "The United States is now rethinking our relationship with the United Nations, and we don't want to be the patsy of the world anymore. That was the message of the last election." said Representative Dana Rohrbacher. The President largely conceded this ground. On June 11, 1995, at an appearance in New Hampshire with then-Speaker of the House Newt Gingrich, President Clinton referred to how "isolationist" the new House Republicans were: "I think they're only reflecting the views of their constituents. That is, people want us to tend to our problems here at home. They don't want us to waste any money overseas. Nothing is more unpopular than doing that now."

Consistent with this interpretation of the public mood, policymakers appeared to have been largely united in the perception that the public would not support U.S. participation in a peacekeeping operation in Bosnia. "The American people will not permit an American army to fight and die there," said Senator Phil Gramm in 1995. And then-Secretary of State Warren Christopher concurred that there "would be no support...among the public for deeper involvement." Polls, however, told a different story. Although the majority of Americans at that time opposed a unilateral U.S. intervention, a substantial number (almost one half of those polled) supported U.S. participation in a multilateral operation. Within a year after U.S. troops went in to help enforce the Dayton peace accord, a strong majority supported the U.S. effort.

On the question of NATO enlargement, opponents asserted that the U.S. public would be unwilling to risk the lives of U.S. troops to defend new members. This argument was ultimately overwhelmed by the extraordinary Senate majority that supported enlargement, accompanied by polls that showed majority support for NATO enlargement.

The assumption that the public would not be enthusiastic about IMF funding was borne out by polls. However, this was apparently prompted more by doubts about its effectiveness than by isolationist attitudes. Among those who paid attention to the issue, there was strong support. Also, after respondents had a chance to deliberate on the issue by hearing a series of strongly stated pro and con arguments, a modest majority favored IMF funding.

The assumption that the public was not supportive of "fast-track" trade negotiating authority for the President was also confirmed by polls. While the public supports free trade in principle, there is substantial concern that other considerations are being ignored in the rush to increase trade. The very term "fast-track" pushed all the wrong buttons. As one discussion group member observed, "Whoever came up with the term "fast-track" didn't do market research. It sounds like plowing ahead without taking important considerations into account."

On China policy there were two competing public opinion profiles—the public as preoccupied with jobs and thus likely to favor expanded trade relations, and the public as highly concerned about human rights and thus likely to oppose expanded trade relations. A July 1998 Gallup poll linking neither jobs nor human rights and taken in the wake of the President's trip to China showed 55 percent opposed to the granting of most favored nation trading rights and 35 percent in favor. According to the same poll, 49 percent felt that relations with China would improve, while 38 percent were not as optimistic. For State Department reorganization, Nunn-Lugar, and the Glenn Amendment, no clear image of the public's views emerged.

In spite of increasingly sophisticated means of gathering and analyzing the views of Americans, it appears that, for the most part, formal public opinion polls play only a modest role in shaping congressional action on foreign policy. Informal soundings of constituents and personal judgments of potential public reactions are much more important. For example, leaders feel constrained by an emerging negative reaction toward U.S. casualties in peacekeeping operations even though polls show that, in the abstract, a majority of the public accepts that risk. Sometimes the debate reflects correct assumptions about public attitudes as measured in polling data. But, in other cases, political leaders seem to discount poll findings, or public opinion plays no role at all.

PARTISANSHIP

The ten case studies revealed a mixed record when it came to partisanship, something of a surprise to members of the discussion group. The recent period in American politics has been so marked by partisan debate, disagreement, mistrust, and recriminations that it might have been expected to have had a more decisive effect on the outcomes of these cases. The group did find points at which debates crossed the line between honest differences and partisan posturing. The debates on Bosnia, UN funding, State Department reorganization, and China all contained partisan elements. But the Nunn-Lugar legislation, NATO enlargement, Glenn Amendment sanctions on India and Pakistan, and eventually State Department reorganization were settled in a bipartisan fashion. And on China, the IMF, fast-track legislation, and foreign affairs resources, the divisions were as evident within the parties as between them.

On the other hand, the end of the Cold War and the dissolution of the Soviet Union appears to have created more room for partisan behavior as opposed to partisan outcomes. Criticizing the President while he is overseas negotiating with foreign counterparts was cited by one discussion group commentator as the epitome of taking stands motivated more by a desire to make the other side look bad than by foreign policy considerations. When there were two opposing superpowers, the costs of such partisanship appeared high and risked being labeled un-American or unpatriotic. There were intense debates, of course, but the main organizing principle behind them was the goal of thwarting Soviet ambitions, whether in Central or Latin America, Africa, or Asia. Today, without such a framework, politicians feel freer to question and critique the fundamental assumptions of administration policies.

For example, in March 1999, when the United States and its NATO allies initiated air attacks against Yugoslavia because of its refusal to halt aggression against Kosovar Albanian civilians, congressional reactions were mixed. Many Members avoided partisan commentaries during the conflict while at the same time raising serious questions about the administration's strategy. Others clearly took the opportunity to criticize the President's handling of the conflict in a more personal and denigrating way. In the end, the Senate passed a resolution authorizing the U.S.-NATO air campaign against the Serbs while the campaign was underway, and the House voted down the same resolution on a tie vote but subsequently approved funds for the mission. So, while the process clearly inspired partisan rhetoric, and one vote in the House broke mainly along party lines, the outcome was congressional approval of funding.

One thing that is clear is that Republican lack of confidence in Bill Clinton has permeated the environment on Capitol Hill. The debacle that led to the ambush and killing of U.S. soldiers in Somalia in the administration's first year reinforced skepticism about the President's decison-making ability in the foreign policy area. On the UN funding issue, Republican concern that President Clinton was relying too heavily on the United Nations and other multilateral institutions was an undercurrent in the issue's consideration. With regard to Kosovo, Republican doubts about the President lay just beneath the surface of their tentative support for the commander in chief while U.S. forces were under fire.

Most discussion group members agreed that the atmosphere became more partisan when, after the 1994 congressional elections, the Republicans gained control of the House of Representatives for the first time in four decades. The Republican victory was accompanied by an exuberance illustrated by the manifesto supported by many Republicans and called the "Contract with America," which laid out domestic and foreign policy objectives, including provisions particularly critical of the United Nations and skeptical about the use of U.S. military forces in multilateral peacekeeping operations. In addition, there was a "payback" factor. Following so many years in the minority, House Republicans were intent on treating the now-minority House Democrats no better than they had been treated. Their new position in the House, matched with Republican control of the Senate, gave Republicans a strong platform from which to challenge the President in all areas of policy.

Clearly, partisanship came into play on the abortion rider that Republicans tried to attach to a number of pieces of foreign affairs legislation. It was also a factor in a second fast-track vote scheduled right before the 1998 elections, and it became apparent at different points during the consideration of agency reorganization and the foreign affairs budget.

But splits within the parties were just as evident in the ten cases as splits between parties. "Some of our most intense foreign policy debates now are intra-party," observed an ISD discussion group adviser to a senior senator. Republicans are split between the free market populists whose antigovernment views carry over into opposing foreign aid and international institutions and the more pragmatic, business-oriented internationalists. The Democratic Party also fragments when it views the world. On economic issues, one group upholds organized labor's concern with labor standards and the environment and opposes free trade. On other issues, some Democrats value the pursuit of human rights and democracy as an overriding interest while others see national security as a primary focus. "Factionalism is more interesting in foreign affairs than partisanship, though both exist and are virulent. The parties are divided into at least two parts, and their two centrist sections are closer to each other on foreign policy than they are to factions in their own parties," noted one ISD discussant.

Redistricting based on the 1990 census has increased the number of districts where the main election battle is fought in the primary between members of the same party. As voter turnout has continued to decline, what used to be called the "wings" of the parties have become stronger factions, and the "odd bedfellow" phenomenon has grown to the point where, on some foreign policy issues, the divisions resemble a multiparty rather than a two-party system.

As a result, despite the strongly partisan environment of recent years, a number of foreign policy issues have been settled with divisions cutting across party lines or in a largely bipartisan manner. With regard to fast track, a majority of Republicans in the House supported a Democratic President, while a majority of Democrats opposed granting the authority. On China, both Democrats and Republicans have criticized the administration's handling of relations. Resolutions intended to punish or criticize China are supported by a conservative group of Republicans who see China as a future adversary, joined by a liberal faction of the Democratic Party reacting to China's human rights policies. The two parties divide along more traditional lines on such issues as allegations that the Chinese government funneled contributions to the Democratic Party, but the Cox Commission report on Chinese espionage was reported out on a bipartisan vote. As for the IMF, it came under criticism from both parties for different reasons, although the conservative wing of the Republican Party was the more active opponent.

On Bosnia, significant numbers of Republicans and Democrats supported lifting the embargo against shipping arms to the Bosnian Muslim forces, in opposition to the President's policy. After the Dayton peace agreement was reached, opinions on the President's approach became more divided by party but, in the end, neither Republicans nor Democrats mounted an effective opposition and subsequently have continued funding the operation.

Three of the cases revealed strong and widespread bipartisan cooperation. The Nunn-Lugar program of assistance to successor states of the former Soviet Union to help keep nuclear technology and weapons from being transferred to third states had not only bipartisan sponsors but also enjoyed wide bipartisan support in the House and the Senate. Close cooperation between Democratic and

Republican staff and senators established a solid core of support for the policy of NATO enlargement. And the lifting of Glenn Amendment sanctions on India and Pakistan was bipartisan. In these three cases, pre-existing substantive differences between Republicans and Democrats were marginal and the ground for decision was effectively prepared by the President and/or by congressional leaders.

INSTITUTIONS AND PROCESSES

Some of the changes in institutional roles and functions that became prominent in the 1990s had been in train for years, but their impact has been magnified by the absence of a foreign policy consensus after the end of the Cold War.

The congressional-executive relationship in foreign policy historically has been conducted through a series of institutions and established procedures based on the Constitution that have been adapted over the course of the nation's history. Accordingly, the President is the commander in chief and has the power to negotiate treaties, receive foreign ambassadors, nominate senior officials, and propose and veto legislation. The Congress, as a whole, has the power to declare war, ratify treaties, regulate foreign trade, and provide the resources for government programs, including funding for diplomacy, foreign aid, and military capabilities. The Senate has the exclusive power to give its advice and consent to the ratification of treaties and to approve presidential nominations. As part of its funding responsibilities, the Congress conducts "oversight" of all government agencies and policies as a way of keeping the executive branch under democratic scrutiny.

Effective conduct of U.S. foreign policy requires that the natural struggle between the branches result in workable decisions rather than deadlock. The ISD group discussed whether or not the institutions and processes intended to make this relationship work are broken.

Several case studies pointed to the fact that congressional consideration of foreign affairs has become increasingly diffused. This phenomenon did not begin in the 1990s. Congressional reforms in the 1970s reduced the power of committee chairmen and began the formal process of spreading leadership of committees and issues to more Members. In addition, the emergence of contemporary problems such as global warming and other environmental concerns, terrorism, and drug trafficking increased the number of issues for which legislative responsibility is divided within the jurisdiction of multiple committees. Adding to the complexity, authority for some aspects of foreign policy in the administration is also spread among a growing number of domestic agencies, complicating both interagency coordination and legislative-executive cooperation.

The information revolution and the speed of international developments reinforce the diffusion. Every Member of Congress can be briefed on breaking international developments by turning on CNN. Pressure from news media for comments on those developments in turn can lead Members to stake out positions on issues before complete information is available.

The Senate Foreign Relations Committee and the House International Relations Committee, the two primary policy authorizing committees for foreign policy issues, have continued to decline in prominence and influence. The group's discussion focused on the fact that other authorizing committees had important stakes in many of the foreign policy issues discussed and that increasing power had accrued to the Senate and House Appropriations committees. One senior Senate committee staffer noted that "[t]he authorizing committees are not getting authorization bills through, not kicking treaties out. Appropriations is having to write more legislation." The influence of the House International Relations Committee has declined in part because of the committee's inability to secure House approval of a foreign aid authorization bill since 1985, one of its principal means to set a tone and provide direction in U.S. foreign policy.

With regard to funding for the IMF, the Banking Committee took a lead role, and hearings were also held by the Agriculture committees and the Joint Economic Committee. On the issue of lifting sanctions against India and Pakistan, several committees, including Government Affairs, Agriculture, Ways and Means, Banking, and Appropriations played key roles. Both Defense committees and the Appropriations committees played important parts on decisions about the commitment of troops to Bosnia. And Ways and Means and Finance committees played leading roles on fast-track trade negotiating authority.

The institutional process seemed to have worked reasonably well in a few cases. In the case of NATO enlargement, the Senate Foreign Relations Committee held extensive hearings and paved the way for debate of the issue on the floor. Appropriations, Armed Services, and other committees held hearings, but Foreign Relations stayed on top of the process. Nunn-Lugar assistance to Russia was handled expeditiously in both houses. With regard to UN funding, the attempt to reach a compromise on the issue came from cooperation between Senate Foreign Relations Committee Chairman Helms and Ranking Minority Member Biden. Different issues arose in the House, where the leadership was unwilling or unable to protect the question from an abortion rider.

Legislative-executive power-sharing in foreign policy requires thorough, effective consultations between the President and the Congress. Even though it is possible to document a formal consultative record for virtually all the cases, the absence of meaningful give-and-take between the branches greatly reduced the impact of formal communications for many of the issues discussed. As one discussion group member observed, "There has been a breakdown in honest communication between the two branches."

Effective consultations, of course, are a two-way street. One discussion group member who had served in the Clinton administration noted that following negotiation of the peace accord for Bosnia "...we would have met with any two Members in a phone booth." This participant reflected on the fact that, for one Bosnia briefing by National Security Advisor Sandy Berger, eight Members were invited, but only one showed up.

Congressional foreign policy institutions work best if the staff and Members of those institutions are well informed and motivated by their perceptions of the national interest. For several years during the 1990s, many Members on both sides of the aisle appeared to have been motivated more by their own political agenda than by a desire to develop an effective, consensual foreign policy. This circumstance led one former Senate staffer to regret that "[p]eople on the Hill do not argue the national interest anymore. They gather a coalition of people who argue a special case together." This said, in a democracy there will always be differing but politically valid interpretations of what is best for the nation. And as one discussant put it, "Debate is a healthy part of our system and can bring about good ideas. Congress provides this valuable contribution."

Finally, perhaps one of the most worrisome emerging issues is whether or not the increasing role of money in politics is becoming part of the problem. A number of discussion group members referred to the fact that the time and effort spent in raising money to get reelected limits the ability of Members to focus on legislative issues, and in particular on complex and seemingly remote foreign policy problems. Hundreds of meetings and thousands of phone calls have to be made to raise money for increasingly expensive media coverage. One political expert and writer, Elizabeth Drew, has noted that "[t]o run a successful Senate race, candidates must now raise an average of $16,000 a week, every week, for six years. A House candidate has to raise $7,100 a week for two years."* One discussion group House staffer noted that his Member's ". . . decision as to whether to get engaged in an issue and how to get engaged comes directly from campaign finance considerations."

Committee assignments are also affected by the need for money. Some committees (Banking, Commerce, and the tax committees, for example) are seen as "cash cows," where important regulatory matters affecting wealthy interests are decided. It is well known that Members of those committees raise money easily no matter what side of the political fence they are on. As one Hill staffer commented, "Members make career development decisions when they decide which committees to sit on. They talk about the money committees, and they don't mean Appropriations."

Service on the Senate Foreign Relations and House International Relations committees is not considered lucrative. Foreign affairs has neither a voting constituency nor financial drawing power—two top concerns when elected officials choose where to spend their time and energy. The constituency problem has always been there, but the money problem has gotten worse in the last decade.

---

*Elizabeth Drew, *The Corruption of American Politics: What Went Wrong and Why* (Birch Lane Press, Carol Publishing Group, N.J., 1990).

4
The Cases and their Impact on U.S. Interests

Perhaps the most difficult issue with which the ISD study group grappled was how to measure success. One group member suggested simply that "the measure of success is whether policies proceed from a truly intelligent debate about the policies and their implications." In any policy battle, there are winners and losers. Compromises never satisfy all parties. Most importantly, a "successful" policy-making process does not guarantee a successful policy when it is applied internationally. Against this background, and based on the discussion group's deliberations, we asked two fundamental questions.

First, we asked, "How well did the process work?"

- Did the two branches of government play the role as outlined in the Constitution or according to procedures based on the Constitution?

- At the end of the process, did the agreed policy have the support of the President and a majority in the Congress?

Then, we asked, "Did the process produce successful policy?"

- Was the outcome relevant to the international circumstances it was intended to affect?

- Did the outcome have the intended effect on U.S. interests?

- Did the outcome have either positive or negative unintended consequences for U.S. interests?

The responses to those questions are surveyed in the paragraphs that follow. The cases reviewed by the discussion group are divided into four categories: security policy, U.S. policy toward China, trade and international finance, and foreign policy tools. In general, we found a higher degree of executive-congressional cooperation in the security policy cases than in the others, and significantly less agreement over resource allocation questions.

SECURITY POLICY

Nunn-Lugar and Soviet Weapons of Mass Destruction

Following the abortive coup attempt against Mikhail Gorbachev's government in August 1991, initial attempts to provide $1 billion in humanitarian and demilitarization support to the Soviet Union ran into criticism that the funds should be spent on domestic programs. At that point, Senators Lugar and Nunn proposed scaling back the proposed aid program and made the case that it was in the U.S. national interest to ensure safe control and/or destruction of weapons of mass destruction in a crumbling and politically chaotic Soviet Union. Members rallied around the initiative, called the "Nunn-Lugar Cooperative Threat Reduction Program," which was passed as an amendment to the 1991 Conventional Forces in Europe Treaty Implementation Act. The amendment authorized the use of $400 million in Department of Defense funds to transport, store, and dismantle nuclear, chemical, and other weapons in the Soviet Union. The President has requested and the Congress, with bipartisan support, has approved similar funding levels in subsequent years. The funds have been spent in Russia, Ukraine, Belarus, and Kazakhstan.

The Nunn-Lugar case demonstrates the potential for the Congress to fill gaps that Members and committees detect in the concepts, programs, or funding proposals of an administration. At the time, President George Bush was under political attack for spending too much time and energy on foreign policy and not enough on domestic requirements. The administration therefore was not well positioned to propose to spend money on the country that so recently had been a U.S. adversary. The initiative did not undermine or oppose Bush administration policy, but rather sought to supplement it with a tool not yet in the President's hands. One discussion group member suggested that Senators Nunn and Lugar used a Harvard study to "...scare the hell out of other Senators about how the Soviet nuclear arsenal could go into the international market place."

Assessment

The institutional process appears to have worked well in this case. Legislation moved very quickly through the process, and its noncontroversial nature appeared to warrant this approach. No committee hearings were held on the original legislation, even though many subsequent hearings have been held on its implementation. The overall impact on U.S. interests has been positive. Thanks in part to Nunn-Lugar assistance, all nuclear weapons have been moved from Ukraine, Kazakhstan, and Belarus to Russia, and other steps to increase the security of the Russian-controlled weapons benefit U.S. national nonproliferation and strategic stability interests. One lesson to be drawn from this case is that congressional initiatives can fill gaps in administration foreign policy approaches, and when such initiatives are designed to attract bipartisan support, they have a good chance of passing the Congress and being signed into law by the President. The case also suggests that fear of dire consequences (in this case wide-open nuclear weapons proliferation) can be a strong incentive to act.

Bosnia, Kosovo, and the Use of Force

The conflict in Bosnia broke out as President Bush was seeking reelection, and the President decided not to involve the United States militarily in the conflict there. The administration hoped that European nations, with a mandate from the United Nations, would be able to stabilize the situation. In the 1992 presidential campaign, Bill Clinton criticized President Bush for his hands-off policy, but then, as President, essentially adopted the same approach. The strategy failed, and conflicts in the Balkans eventually came to dominate congressional-legislative interactions on use of force issues during the second Clinton administration. But Clinton's experiences with foreign intervention during his first term—in Somalia and Haiti—had a major impact on the congressional-legislative relationship over the U.S. decision to send military forces to Bosnia.

The problems encountered and lessons learned from prior experiences, particularly in Somalia, helped shape the administration's approach to its decision to send troops to police a negotiated peace in Bosnia at the end of 1995. Following the disaster in Somalia, the administration adopted severe constraints on its intervention policy, incorporated in Presidential Decision Directive (PDD) 25 in the spring of 1994. PDD 25 reflected the impact of congressional views on foreign policy and included many perspectives that had been expressed by Members. PDD 25 made a number of promises desired by Members of Congress, including a commitment that an intervention would have a clear exit strategy.

When the warring parties in Bosnia reached a U.S.-brokered accord in the fall of 1995, the President had no choice but to honor his pledge to help enforce such an accord. However, he knew that the Congress would likely be unenthusiastic about such an operation. Therefore, he waited to state his intention to request an expression of support from the Congress for U.S. participation in a Bosnian peacekeeping force until October 19, 1995, after military planners had already begun preparing the operation. At this point, it was clear that U.S. nonparticipation would lead to a collapse of the entire peace process.

The administration was correct in believing that there would be substantial congressional skepticism about U.S. involvement in Bosnia. It argued that U.S. rejection of a role in Bosnia could mean the end of NATO. It also maintained that the President did not require congressional approval to join in the operation. Nevertheless, within ten days of Clinton's statement, the House passed a nonbinding resolution (H.R. 247) prohibiting U.S. armed forces from being deployed to enforce the peace agreement until the Congress had approved the deployment. But congressional attempts to ban funding for the operation failed. Presented with mixed signals, the administration went ahead without seeking or receiving congressional support for the operation.

The administration had promised that the initial operation would not last more than a year, but Bosnia was far from settled at the end of the year. So the administration ended the first mission and developed a second one, a commitment to be reviewed periodically.

Congressional opposition to U.S. involvement in Bosnia softened over time because the United States took no combat casualties, and the operation seemed to have helped stabilize the situation. When the crisis in neighboring Kosovo erupted in 1998, some Members of Congress, including notably the much-respected Vietnam War veteran Senator John McCain, argued for a fully developed, U.S.-led NATO offensive against Serbia at a time when the administration was limiting the engagement to a high-level air operation. The Kosovo mission faced significant skepticism and some opposition in the Congress but ended before any U.S. casualties were taken and before congressional patience ran out.

The most important aspect of the congressional-executive relationship over the Balkan operations was the clear congressional skepticism about the Clinton administration's ability to conceive and conduct effective military operations, combined with an unwillingness either to actively support or cut off funding for such operations.

Assessment

Institutional processes did not work well. There was insufficient dialogue between the President and the Congress in advance of the decision to send U.S. troops to help implement the peace in Bosnia. Then, the Congress decided not to approve or disapprove the mission but only to support U.S. troops. The policy itself, at least to date, can be said to be a success, even though the end of the story may be years away. The peace accord in Bosnia is being implemented, the American people have come to support the U.S. role in that process, and U.S. troop numbers have been reduced and no combat casualties have been incurred. With regard to Kosovo, the Congress followed a pattern similar to Bosnia, except in this case some Members actually argued for more assertive use of U.S. military capabilities. The institutional tendency of the Congress was to criticize but not to take responsibility for turning on or turning off the use of military force. U.S. engagement in the Balkan conflicts clearly reveals the leadership tendency to avoid U.S. casualties even at the risk of undermining the foreign policy goals or military effectiveness of an operation.

NATO Enlargement

At the end of the Cold War, the new democratic governments of most Central and East European states that had been members of the Soviet-dominated Warsaw Pact began lobbying for membership in NATO. The United States and the other NATO allies first attempted to defer decisions on the issue because of the many complications involved, including concerns about the cost to the Alliance of admitting new members and the risk of complicating relations with the new government of Russia, which opposed enlarging NATO.

In 1994, President Clinton decided that simply offering such governments cooperation with NATO through programs like the Partnership for Peace was insufficient. He embraced the membership bid of the Polish government and opened the door to consideration of other candidates as well.

At the same time, bipartisan support for NATO enlargement was developing in the House and Senate, which over several years passed legislation intended to support the membership desires of Central and East European democracies. The 1994 House Republican "Contract with America" strongly supported NATO enlargement. Behind the scenes, bipartisan staff work, supported by Clinton administration officials, began orienting this support toward the day when the Senate might be asked to give its advice and consent to new democracies joining the Alliance.

At the NATO summit in Madrid in July 1997, three countries (the Czech Republic, Hungary, and Poland) were invited to join NATO. Several Members of the Senate and House were included in the U.S. delegation to the meeting. By the end of the year these three countries had negotiated the terms of their membership with NATO, and the ratification process began in 1998.

The Senate held a sometimes-contentious debate stretched out over several weeks in the late spring of 1998, ultimately producing a majority of eighty to nineteen, well over the two-thirds majority of Senators present and voting to consent to the accession of the three countries to the Treaty of Washington (the North Atlantic Treaty).

Although President Clinton's advocacy of enlargement was interpreted in part as politically motivated (critics said his 1994 advocacy of enlargement was intended to help him in his 1996 bid for a second term), his ultimate opponent in that election, Senator Robert Dole, was an equally strong supporter of enlargement. The debate and vote in the Senate were bipartisan, with supporters and opponents including both Democrats and Republicans.

Assessment

The President and several Members of Congress played requisite leading roles, and the appropriate oversight committees fulfilled their responsibilities. Opposing arguments were taken into full consideration. The process, therefore, worked well. The outcome was consistent with the President's policy, the majority will in the Congress was honored, and the policy was supported by U.S. public opinion. The decision negatively affected relations with Russia, and it is still too early to determine whether that will be a short- or long-term consequence. This case demonstrated that, even at a time when the Republican majority in the Congress held deep suspicions about President Clinton and his foreign policy, a convergence of views, fortified by intensive executive-legislative consultations and effective special interest lobbies, was capable of producing an outcome supported by the administration and a substantial bipartisan majority in the Congress.

U.S. Policy Toward China

Few issues better illuminate the complexity of policy-making in the post-Cold War era and the challenges to reaching executive-legislative agreement than the issue of Sino-U.S. relations.

During the 1970s and 1980s China and the United States had a common adversary in the Soviet Union. In addition, there was an exaggerated optimism among some Americans about the direction of political evolution in China. The collapse of the Soviet Union and the 1989 Tiananmen massacre effectively removed what were for Americans essential underpinnings of the relationship. The United States has important national interests at stake in its relationship with China, including China's role in Asian peace and stability, military cooperation and arms sales, weapons proliferation and Chinese policy toward Taiwan, U.S.-China bilateral trade and the terms for China's membership in the World Trade Organization, issues concerning transfer of technology, China's protection of intellectual property rights, and questions concerning Chinese human rights practices and religious persecution.

Sino-U.S. relations after the 1989 Tiananmen killings faced extensive press scrutiny, interest group activism, and congressional attention. President Bush was forced into regular battles with the Congress over China policy. The annual renewal of most-favored-nation treatment for China became the congressional vehicle of choice to hold the executive branch accountable.

The battles between the branches continued during the Clinton administration. President Clinton intensified his problems by reversing his stance toward Beijing. In 1993 he linked renewal of most-favored-nation treatment to progress on human rights. A year later he effectively dropped this linkage. By his second term, President Clinton was speaking optimistically about moving "toward a constructive strategic partnership" between the two countries. Recently, the relationship has fallen on hard times in light of allegations that China engaged in espionage against the United States, the accidental U.S. bombing of the Chinese embassy in Belgrade, and violent Chinese demonstrations outside the U.S. embassy in Beijing.

The number of "players" on these issues is significant. Interest group involvement is high from corporate lobbyists to human rights groups. Virtually every executive branch agency has a China interest. Many congressional committees have examined one or more aspects of the bilateral relationship.

Congressional involvement in Sino-U.S. relations has been episodic—very intense at times and largely absent at others. The Congress has not blocked most-favored-nation renewal during the two Clinton terms but has passed a stream of legislation critical of China. Representative Lee Hamilton, in a November 17, 1998, speech at the Center for Strategic and International Studies in Washington, D.C., noted that, as the 105th Congress closed, the House passed nine anti-China bills, expressing displeasure with Chinese policies on everything from human rights to nonproliferation. Hamilton pointed out that "[n]o hearings were held on any of the bills. The administration was not consulted about the impact the bills could have on U.S.-China relations, nor on how they fit into our overall policy. Indeed, they seemed designed mainly for political purposes." A member of the discussion group who is intimately familiar with congressional handling of China issues labeled the Hill's approach to China, "chaotic, disorganized, and dysfunctional."

An interesting feature of the congressional consideration of China is that it frequently does not break down along clearly defined partisan lines. On many occasions, liberal Democrats have combined with conservative Republicans in criticizing China and U.S. policies toward China.

Assessment

The Congress has frequently diverged sharply from the executive branch during both the Bush and Clinton administrations. It remains to be seen whether or not the outcome of this interaction will benefit U.S. interests. This issue is far from concluded, and the struggle to find the appropriate balance among a variety of commercial, human rights, nuclear nonproliferation, and strategic interests in in the relationship with China will clearly continue into the next decade. It will be difficult for the next administration to develop a consensus, given widely divergent views and conflicting goals. But the consequences of getting China policy wrong could be so devastating and the benefits of getting it right so positive that intensive executive-legislative consultations and open dialogue on China policy issues should be a top priority.

TRADE AND INTERNATIONAL FINANCE

Fast-track Trade Negotiating Authority

From its creation in the Trade Act of 1974 to 1994, fast-track negotiating authority has been granted by the Congress to every President who has requested it. Fast-track authority allows the President to negotiate trade agreements that are not subject to amendment by the Congress and that must be voted up or down within a given time period. This is an issue that does not necessarily produce partisan divisions but certainly can be subject to them, depending on the circumstances. It is also an issue in which the Senate tends to be more supportive of granting such authority to the President than the House. In any case, the President has to demonstrate strong commitment in order to produce required majorities for fast-track authority, particularly because such legislation requires the Congress to compromise some of its constitutional prerogatives in order to strengthen the President's position in international negotiations.

The Congress extended fast-track authority to President Clinton in 1993 to allow him to complete the Uruguay Round of negotiations under the terms of the General Agreement on Tariffs and Trade. Since 1994, however, the Congress has not extended fast-track authority to President Clinton.

In 1997, fast-track legislation was thought to be within a few votes of passage in the House, but the White House and the congressional leadership failed to put the final majority together and the measure was put aside. A former senior congressional staffer observed that "[b]oth parties needed to pick up ten votes the weekend before the 1997 vote. By Sunday night, the Republicans were up to 168 or 169 and had picked up eight or nine votes. The Democrats had picked up none. I don't think the President was working that weekend."

When fast-track authority was brought up again in 1998, just prior to midterm congressional elections and in the middle of a partisan debate around the Clinton impeachment proceedings, the measure fell in a vote largely along party lines.

An important World Trade Organization ministerial meeting to set the ground rules for the next round of international trade negotiations opened in November 1999, and President Clinton's hand remained weakened by the lack of authority to negotiate under fast-track authority. The case has illustrated the critical roles that partisanship and effective presidential leadership (or lack thereof) can play in the conduct of U.S. foreign policy.

Assessment

The Congress may have successfully represented sectoral and other interests that feared being hurt by further trade-liberalizing legislation, but most ISD discussion group members believed that U.S. foreign economic policy would benefit from fast-track legislation, and so the outcome was judged a failure. The President did not devote sufficient political capital and energy to gain passage, in contrast to his hard and successful personal efforts to garner support for NAFTA. The process, therefore, was lacking the key ingredient of focused presidential leadership. This case demonstrated that effective White House lobbying and arm-twisting can be critical even in a case where there is already substantial congressional support—in this case particularly among the Republican majority.

Increasing the International Monetary Fund Quota

Increasing the U.S. quota for the International Monetary Fund was a highly contentious issue in the 105th Congress. The Asian financial crisis and the collapse of the Russian ruble both informed and inflamed the debate. IMF prescriptions and loans during the crisis raised questions and caused misgivings about its role and effectiveness. Some Members argued that IMF funds supported "crony capitalism" or inefficient statism in Southeast Asia and other developing areas. Other Members argued that IMF funds were going to countries with poor human rights records or insufficient labor and environmental standards. Still others argued that IMF remedies were too austere, causing rather than solving problems. Both conservatives and liberals argued that the IMF should be reformed to make its decision-making processes more transparent.

IMF funding comes up for approval every five to six years, and congressional interest in the organization in intervening years is minimal. Because institutional knowledge of the IMF and its purposes and programs is weak, congressional opponents of IMF funding are often able to dominate a debate. U.S. funding occurs as an exchange of financial assets and does not have to be offset by a cut in domestic spending under the agreed budgetary guidelines. But quota increases require congressional approval.

In the end, the argument that the United States needed to support the IMF's role in providing stability to unsettled currencies, especially in a crisis, prevailed. Despite reservations and after considerable airing in various congressional forums, the Congress did approve IMF funding in the Omnibus Appropriations Act for fiscal year 1999, which was signed into law by President Clinton on October 21, 1998.

Some of the early sparring on the IMF legislation included attempts in the House to attach anti-abortion-related language denying the use of U.S. funds to finance foreign family-planning organizations. The final bill included no controversial language on family planning, human rights, or other "secondary" issues. It did condition IMF funding on the Treasury Department's certification that the major IMF donors agree to various IMF reforms. These included greater transparency and a commitment to charge higher interest rates in certain short-term crisis situations. The legislation also included reporting requirements and a U.S. General Accounting Office annual audit of the IMF. These and other measures made it clear that the Congress wanted to play a more active role in the shaping of future U.S. policy toward the IMF. This outcome was seen as positive.

Assessment

In the group's judgment, President Clinton, like Presidents Bush and Reagan before him, made little effort to communicate with the

52 The Cases and their Impact on U.S. Interests

Congress on IMF-related issues during years when a quota increase was not pending. Nor has the Congress pursued international financial issues in a sustained and effective way. Therefore, except in a few spots on the Hill, mainly in the banking committees, there is not extensive knowledge about whether U.S. national interests are served by IMF programs. Nonetheless, the outcome was successful.

FOREIGN POLICY TOOLS

Resources for Foreign Affairs

At a time when the Congress has been focused on balancing the federal budget, it is no surprise that funding for foreign affairs activities has been a source of tension between the President and the Congress. The State Department and the foreign policy establishment have no important financial backers, powerful lobby groups, or natural constituencies among voters to help them make their case to Members of Congress. Foreign assistance has never been popular on the Hill and, with the Cold War over, one previous rationale—stopping the Soviet Union—has vanished. One ISD working group member pointed out that even though foreign affairs spending accounts for less than one percent of the overall budget, it constitutes approximately 7.5 percent of funds that are available for discretionary spending if defense spending and politically untouchable domestic spending is put aside. Another member pointed out that, although total amounts for foreign affairs funding may have declined, it has taken a consistent slice out of a shrinking discretionary pie.

This case study looked particularly at the authorization and appropriation process during the 105th Congress (1997–98). The focus was on the so-called Function 150 of the federal budget, which includes operation of foreign affairs agencies, foreign aid, and technical assistance; U.S. contributions to international financial institutions and multilateral organizations; trade promotion activities; security assistance and military sales to foreign governments; and humanitarian and refugee assistance. Since 1985, funding for these functions has declined, although the percentage depends on the year chosen as the base. The State Department has claimed a 50 percent reduction in the last fifteen years. An independent ISD study found that bilateral and multilateral aid levels fell by approximately thirty percent between 1991 and 1996 while the operating budget of the

U.S. Information Agency fell by 20 percent, the Agency for International Development's operating budget fell by 5 percent, and the State Department's budget was held to zero growth at a time when the Department was opening more than twenty new embassies in the former Soviet Union and Eastern Europe.

In the 105th Congress, once again there was no authorization bill for either the State Department or foreign aid. Abortion-related restrictions on international family planning funds (Mexico City language) added in June 1998 doomed the State Department authorization bill, which did survive conference but was then vetoed by the President. Appropriated funds, with a waiver eliminating the requirement for authorization, were included in the Omnibus Bill, signed into law on October 21, 1998. The bill contained $12.8 billion in foreign aid, $750 million less than the President had requested. The Omnibus Bill also contained language reorganizing the foreign affairs agencies as well as $475 million in partial payment of UN arrears, but since the UN funds were subject to authorization, the dues could not be paid.

Assessment

The executive and legislative branches share the blame for the continuous decline in the foreign affairs budget. The White House has submitted bare-bones budgets to the Congress, and the Congress has cut them further. The successful congressional move to reorganize the foreign affairs agencies was motivated more by a desire to spend less money on foreign affairs than by a strong desire to match foreign policy goals with resources adequate to pursue them. Some cooperation between the branches has been useful. The congressional initiative to move ever scarcer foreign aid away from the Camp David entitlements for Israel and Egypt and toward Africa and Latin America was welcomed by the executive branch, although new Middle East commitments may put this agreement in jeopardy. And the Congress has increased funding for overseas security after the embassy bombings in Africa, albeit to be offset by cuts in other foreign affairs areas. But both bilateral and multilateral assistance has decreased over the decade, diplomatic presence has thinned, and public diplomacy efforts abroad have been substantially reduced. The next administration and Congress, therefore, will be challenged to make a better match between foreign policy goals and resources.

State Department Reorganization

The reorganization of the foreign affairs bureaucracy was addressed by two Congresses, beginning with the 104th, midway through President Clinton's first term, and concluding when, on October 21, 1998, President Clinton signed into law the Omnibus Consolidated and Emergency Supplemental Appropriations Act for 1999 (H.R. 4328). The legislation abolished the Arms Control and Disarmament Agency, the U.S. Information Agency, and the International Development Cooperation Agency, placing the functions and responsibilities of these agencies under the State Department. In addition, the bill reorganized the Agency for International Development.

The dynamic that eventually led to the reorganization included a number of factors, starting with Vice President Al Gore's National Performance Review initiative. Gore's project initially included proposals developed within the administration and credited to Secretary of State Warren Christopher that would have consolidated foreign policy management, nonproliferation, foreign assistance, international exchanges, and foreign broadcasting under a new "Department of International Relations." When Gore's commission ultimately rejected this suggestion in January 1995, concluding that ACDA, AID, and USIA were "essential vehicles for the accomplishment of their missions," Senator Jesse Helms, chairman of the Senate Foreign Relations Committee, forwarded his own proposals, reflecting many of the original consolidation ideas.

At first, the administration rejected Senator Helms' proposal, and the issue divided along party lines, continuing for many months during the 104th Congress.

The conflict went on until the beginning of Clinton's second term, when, as part of an attempt to forge a more constructive relationship with Senator Helms, the new Secretary of State, Madeleine Albright, struck a deal with Senator Helms to pursue a consolidation plan through a cooperative approach. This accord did not eliminate all partisan differences over the issue but did, eventually, produce a reorganization of the foreign policy bureaucracy.

Assessment

Final judgment on the impact on U.S. interests will await more experience with the new organizational arrangements that are just now emerging. The executive-legislative negotiating process was uneven, with the administration first opposing and then supporting the reorganization. The leaders and employees of the organizations that were to be merged with the State Department opposed the move. In particular, U.S. Information Agency employees questioned whether they could effectively perform their mission of presenting a balanced and culturally diverse image of the United States to the world's public working within an agency (the State Department) whose first mission is to pursue U.S. interests as interpreted in the policies of the current President and administration. Whether or not this will become a serious problem remains to be seen. If reorganization results in a more streamlined foreign affairs bureaucracy that can be efficiently managed and sufficiently funded, the effort will have been successful. The case did yield an outcome on which the President and the Congress agreed, perhaps in itself a step forward for U.S. interests.

Glenn Amendment of 1994
(sanctions to deter India and Pakistan from detonating nuclear weapons)

This case was studied as one example of congressional-executive interaction on a sanctions issue. The story of the Glenn Amendment of 1994 goes back twenty years to the initial Indian test of a nuclear weapon in 1974. During the intervening years, successive Presidents and the Congress have agreed to try to deter nuclear proliferation in South Asia by threatening sanctions against the two potential proliferators. The issue has never been particularly partisan. Institutionally, however, there has been tension between the two branches over the President's ability to waive application of sanctions. The 1994 Glenn Amendment made sanctions mandatory, giving the President no discretion in deciding when or whether to impose sanctions if India were to resume or Pakistan were to begin testing nuclear devices.

When India conducted five underground nuclear tests on May 11 and 13 of 1999, President Clinton reported to the Congress that he was imposing the economic and military sanctions mandated by the Glenn Amendment. After Pakistan followed with five tests of its own on May 28 and an additional test on May 30, President Clinton announced his intent to apply the same sanctions on Pakistan.

The fact that India and Pakistan had both decided to test demonstrated that the threat of U.S. sanctions had not overridden national security considerations in either country. Implementing the sanctions would no longer deter, but punish. The argument was made that following through on the threat was important to the credibility of U.S. nuclear nonproliferation policy.

A counter argument, however, based on U.S. domestic considerations, emerged very quickly, capturing the support of Republicans and Democrats, the Congress, and the administration. While India and Pakistan had demonstrated they were willing to risk the imposition of sanctions, the main burden of the sanctions in the United States fell on American farmers and businessmen with trade ties to the two countries. Almost immediately, under the urging of U.S. farm associations and business interests, the application of sanctions was temporarily limited.

The decision to waive most of the sanctions was a clear example of the President and the Congress working together toward a common purpose. Both institutions abandoned the sanctions in response to domestic concerns and also in recognition of the shortcomings of imposing sanctions unilaterally.

This case makes an interesting contrast to the Helms-Burton sanctions legislation (imposing sanctions against firms doing business with Cuba), whose burden fell largely on non-U.S. firms. Even though the Helms-Burton legislation allowed the President to waive sanctions if such action was deemed in the U.S. national security interest, the legislation seriously soured relations with U.S. allies and convinced some observers outside the United States that unilateralist U.S. behavior was a growing threat to the international system.

Assessment

The ISD group's judgment on the institutional processes was mixed. The Congress and the administration worked generally toward some common objectives. Close congressional-executive cooperation prompted the Congress to adopt legislation that sought to deter nuclear proliferation but provided temporary flexibility to the President regarding application of sanctions. The waiver authority, desired by the President for foreign policy reasons, was strongly favored by U.S. commercial and agricultural interests. The outcome was based largely on bipartisan and congressional-executive agreement. Some group members argued, however, that reversing years of nonproliferation policy was a mistake and that future threats of reprisals would not be taken seriously. Others called it a success—a situation in which the legislative and executive branches cooperated successfully to adapt a failed policy to changing circumstances.

Funding for the United Nations

U.S. failure to pay its dues to the United Nations in a timely manner has been one of the most serious embarrassments for the Clinton administration's foreign policy. The issue developed out of conservative Republican displeasure with the United Nations in general and a variety of UN programs in particular, especially peacekeeping operations. Inability to resolve the issue over several years of negotiations undermined U.S. leadership in the UN and diminished the image of the United States among many governments, including those of close allies. It also weakened the position of United Nations Secretary General Kofi Annan, who, with the promise of U.S. action on the arrears issue, pushed for reform of the UN, let people go, got a no-growth budget approved, and then did not get the arrears paid.

The Clinton administration has regularly included funding for UN arrears in its budget submissions to the Congress. The issue remained unresolved, however, despite a bipartisan effort in the Senate by Senate Foreign Relations Chairman Helms and Ranking Minority Member Biden to produce a compromise outcome. In 1997, even though there were different UN, administration, and congressional estimates of the amounts due, a settlement package was negotiated that passed the Senate by a vote of ninety to five. However, in conference with the House, "Mexico City" language on abortion programs was added at the behest of the House conferees. The Senate conferees, and eventually the Senate as a whole by a one-vote margin, accepted the House language. But the White House balked at working out any compromise on the Mexico City language. As one discussion group member observed, "The White House had already made a commitment not to bargain away its position on family planning on the fast-track trade negotiating issue; it surely wasn't going to do it for UN reform."

Failure to resolve the issue meant that the United States missed the opportunity to clear up the arrearage issue in advance of the end-of-1997 UN budget decisions. A chance was lost to begin the process of improving the U.S. reputation at the UN, as was the opportunity to get countries like China, who underpay in the current UN financing scheme, to increase their contribution and lower that of the United States. Meanwhile, the administration agreed to the reorganization of the foreign affairs agencies, a move that had previously been packaged with resolution of the UN arrears issue.

Assessment

Neither the process nor the policy could be regarded as a success. The UN dues impasse illustrated the importance of presidential and congressional leadership in rising above what is a controversial issue, with two strong domestic lobbies, to resolve a deadlock that can damage U.S. international interests. Despite a good working relationship between Senators Biden and Helms on the UN issue and administration efforts to compromise on UN reform issues, deadlock occurred. The Congress insisted on using important foreign policy legislation as a vehicle for unrelated legislation, and the White House refused to budge on compromise language on the abortion issue. The gridlock substantially weakened U.S. influence at the United Nations and undermined the Secretary General, who led a significant reform effort in the UN as part of his understanding that this would produce U.S. payments.

The impasse was finally broken in November 1999, after this project completed its work. The Mexico City abortion language was included in the funding, but the legislation also allowed for a presidential waiver.

5
Conclusions

The foreign policy road between Capitol Hill and the White House is full of potential potholes, any one of which can block cooperation and produce deadlock. Some of these barriers to cooperation are institutional, based on the constitutionally created tension between presidential and congressional prerogatives in foreign policy. Some are partisan, reflecting the constant struggle between the two parties for votes and, ultimately, control of the government and its policies. Others are more idiosyncratic, based on the personalities and performance of the President, the President's top foreign policy lieutenants, and congressional leaders.

At the end of the 1990s, there is a persistent distrust between the two branches whose origins date back to the Vietnam War. That institutional obstacle to cooperation has been exacerbated by the fact that, for most of the last decade, divided government has added another competitive layer to the legislative-executive relationship. And, the particularly troubled relationship between President Clinton and the Republican leadership in the Congress has added several more obstacles to cooperation. For over half the membership of the Congress, Bill Clinton is the only President with whom they have worked. Other unique factors helped produce the troubling tendencies of the 1990s, including the end of the Cold War and the U.S. budget deficit.

Our review of these ten foreign policy cases revealed a mixed record in terms of outcome and provided evidence for a troubling decline in the quality of executive-legislative communication. The relationship includes substantial continuity with previous decades, but with some new stresses and disturbing discontinuities. This does not necessarily mean that the trends in the 1990s toward reduced focus on and constrained resources for U.S. foreign policy will carry over into the next century. With a decade of experience in coping with challenges to U.S. interests in the post-Cold War world, a public that is for the most part ready to be led in support of U.S. international involvement, the promise of budget surpluses for several years to come, and a new President and Congress to be elected in 2000, more reassuring trends could well emerge in the early years of the new millennium.

Such an optimistic scenario requires, however, that leaders in both branches and parties seek to remedy problems that have plagued the relationship during the past decade. More and better presidential leadership must be matched by a higher quality of statesmanship among congressional leaders. The nation needs Members of Congress who are as serious about foreign policy decisions as they are about important domestic policy issues. In the long run, the nation's domestic and foreign policy interests are cut from the same cloth, and a better informed, more aware Congress can help ensure that American democracy remains safe and its interests secure in the twenty-first century.

Discussion Group Participants

Graeme Bannerman served on the Senate Foreign Relations Committee staff and as its staff director in the 1980s. He is currently president of Bannerman & Associates.

Jeff Bergner worked for many years for Senator Richard Lugar and served as staff director of the Senate Foreign Relations Committee. He is currently president of the firm of Bergner & Bockorny.

James Bond began his twenty-six year congressional career in 1972 and served most recently on the Foreign Operations Subcommittee of the Senate Appropriations Committee. He is now executive vice president of Collins & Company.

Monica Chavez worked on the Hill for eighteen years, first with the Senate Foreign Relations Committee and more recently with the Senate Armed Services Committee. She is now vice president of Pacific Sierra Research.

William Danvers served eight years in the House, four years in the Senate, and four years in the executive branch working in the White House as a special assistant to the President. He is now associated with the firm of Griffin, Johnson, Dover & Stewart.

NOTE: Members of the discussion group were not asked to sign the final report. The report, however, draws heavily on the deliberations of the group.

Discussion Group Participants

Terry Deibel has served in the State Department, the Defense Department, and the Executive Office of the President. He is currently Professor of National Strategy at the National War College

Louis Fisher has been with the Congressional Research Service since 1970, where he now serves as a senior specialist. He served as research director of the House Iran-Contra Committee in 1987.

Charles Flickner began his congressional career in 1974 with Senator Ed Muskie on the Senate Budget Committee. He is currently serving on the staff of the Foreign Operations Subcommittee of the House Appropriations Committee.

Alison Fortier worked on the House Foreign Affairs Committee and on the National Security Council staff. She is currently with Lockheed Martin Corporation.

Alton Frye worked for years with Senator Ed Brooke and has continued to consult with a number of Members of Congress, both Democrat and Republican, from his current position as Presidential Senior Fellow at the Council on Foreign Relations.

Peter Galbraith has divided his career between the legislative and executive branches. Most recently, he served as U.S. ambassador to Croatia. He is currently lecturing at the National War College.

Barry Hager worked on the staff of the House Banking Committee. He is currently practicing law in Washington, D.C.

Robert Hathaway worked on the staff of the House International Relations Committee for more than a dozen years. He is now the director of the Asia program at the Woodrow Wilson International Center for Scholars.

Allison Hiltz is a legislative aide to Senator Mitch McConnell.

Lorelei Kelly worked for Congresswoman Elizabeth Furse as director of the Security for a New Century congressional staff study group.

Stephen Kull is the director of the Program on International Policy Attitude in Washington, D.C., and is the author of *Misreading the Pub-*

lic: The Myth of a New Isolationism, published in the summer of 1999 by The Brookings Institution.

Carol Lancaster has held several positions in the executive branch, most recently as deputy administrator of the U.S. Agency for International Development. She has also served on the staffs of Senator Dick Clark and Congressman David Obey. She is now director of the Master of Science in Foreign Service program at Georgetown University.

Mary Locke worked for Senator Charles Percy on both his personal staff and on the Senate Foreign Relations Committee when he was chairman. She is currently with Georgetown University's Institute for the Study of Diplomacy.

Princeton Lyman has spent most of his professional life in the foreign service representing the United States overseas. He also served in Washington as assistant secretary of State for International Organizations. He is now a senior fellow at the Overseas Development Council.

George Cranwell Montgomery worked for years with Senator Howard Baker during the senator's years as majority leader and served more recently as U.S. ambassador to Oman. He is now associated with the firm Baker, Donelson, Bearman, & Caldwell.

Douglas Norell has worked on Capitol Hill for twenty years on both House and Senate staffs. He is now the senior foreign policy adviser to Senator Byron Dorgan.

Gardner Peckham first worked for the Congress in 1977 and later served in the State Department and the National Security Council. He was most recently assistant to the speaker of the house, Newt Gingrich. He is now managing director of the firm Black, Kelly, Scruggs & Healey.

Ed Rice spent seventeen years on Capitol Hill, including six years on the staff of the House International Relations Committee. He is currently president of the Coalition for Employment Through Exports.

John Roots worked on Capitol Hill for several years for Senator Ted Stevens, chairman of the Senate Appropriations Committee. He is now a partner with the firm of Chambers, Conlon & Hartwell.

Discussion Group Participants

Alison Rosenberg served on the personal staff of Senator Charles Percy and on the Senate Foreign Relations Committee staff. She also held senior positions in the State Department and USAID, and served on the National Security Council staff. She is currently a staff member at the World Bank.

Andrew Semmel left the Pentagon in 1985 to work on the Senate Foreign Relations Committee staff. He now serves on Senator Richard Lugar's personal staff as a senior foreign policy advisor.

Stanley Sloan recently retired after twenty-four years with the Congressional Research Service, which followed several years of military and executive branch service. He now works as an independent consultant.

Nancy Stetson has worked for eighteen years on Capitol Hill and is currently on the staff of the Senate Foreign Relations Committee.

Seth Tillman worked for sixteen years with Senator William Fulbright as a member of the staff of the Senate Foreign Relations Committee. He is currently a distinguished research professor of diplomacy at the School of Foreign Service at Georgetown University.

Pat Towell has covered the Hill as a reporter for the *Congressional Quarterly* for twenty-three years. He is a Georgetown University graduate.

Mike Van Dusen began his twenty-seven year congressional career in 1971 and served most recently with Congressmen Lee Hamilton as chief of the minority staff of the House International Relations Committee. He is currently deputy director of the Woodrow Wilson International Center for Scholars.

Chris Walker began his congressional career in the House in 1986. More recently, he served for four years on the Senate Foreign Relations Committee staff working with Senator Jesse Helms, the chairman. He is now working on the Foreign Operations Subcommittee of the House Appropriations Committee.

Casimir Yost worked on the personal staff of Senator Charles Mathias and on the staff of the Senate Foreign Relations Committee. He is currently Director of the Institute for the Study of Diplomacy.

Georgetown's School of Foreign Service graduate students *Marcos Mandojana, Thomas Kim, Kevin Ritz, Michael Garcia,* and *Simon Limage* also participated in the working group as researchers and rapporteurs.

COMMENTATORS

Jeremy Rosner, vice president of Greenberg Quinlan Research, managed the administration's NATO enlargement effort on the Hill and is the author of *The New Tug of War: Congress, the Executive Branch and National Security* published by the Carnegie Endowment in 1995.

John Schall formerly was Senator Robert Dole's chief budget advisor and the chief of staff in the Labor Department. He was executive director of the Advocacy for UN Interests Abroad project and narrowly lost a bid for election to the Congress in 1994 from Michigan's 13th District.

Dov Zakheim is the chief executive officer of SPC International Corp. He is a former deputy under-secretary of defense. He is the author of *Congress and National Security in the Post-Cold War Era*, published by the Nixon Center in October 1998.